# WHAT WE NEED IS HERE

*Practicing
the Heart of*
CHRISTIAN
SPIRITUALITY

## L. ROGER OWENS

UPPER
ROOM BOOKS®
NASHVILLE

Upper Room Books® website: books.upperroom.org

Upper Room®, Upper Room Books®, and design logos are trademarks owned by The Upper Room®, Nashville, Tennessee. All rights reserved.

Scripture quotations not otherwise noted are from the New Revised Standard Version Bible, copyright 1989 National Council of the Churches of Christ in the United States of America. Used by permission. All rights reserved.

Scripture quotations marked KJV are taken from the King James Version.

Lines from "The Wild Geese" copyright © 2012 by Wendell Berry from *New Collected Poems*. Reprinted by permission of Counterpoint.

Cover design: Bruce Gore | Gore Studio, Inc.
Cover photo: iStock images
Interior design and layout: PerfecType, Nashville

LIBRARY OF CONGRESS CATALOGING-IN-PUBLICATION DATA
Owens, L. Roger, 1975-
  What we need is here : practicing the heart of Christian spirituality / L. Roger Owens.
    pages cm
  ISBN 978-0-8358-1510-9 (print) — ISBN 978-0-8358-1511-6 (epub)—ISBN 978-0-8358-1530-7 (mobi)
1. Spiritual life—Christianity. I. Title.
  BV4501.3.O96 2015
  248.4—dc23

                                                        2014047971

# Praise for
## *What We Need Is Here*

Rare is the book that will change your feelings. You're holding one such book in your hands. Roger Owens's work is wise, gentle, funny, and holy.

—Jason Byassee
Butler Chair in Homiletics and Biblical Interpretation
Vancouver School of Theology

Roger Owens takes us to the heart of Christian spirituality in this affirmative, practical guide. With well-formed biblical wisdom and a warm pastor's heart, Roger gives us wise guidance on the ways we can meet and be met by a living, loving God.

—Will Willimon
Retired United Methodist bishop
Professor of the Practice of Christian Ministry
Duke Divinity School

For my mother,

GAYLE OWENS

# CONTENTS

# ACKNOWLEDGMENTS

Some of the material in this book began as lectures for The Upper Room Academy for Spiritual Formation. I'm grateful to the several retreat leaders who invited me to present and especially to Johnny Sears for his leadership of the Academy.

I am also grateful to the folks at Upper Room Books for their work shepherding this book through production. Rita Collett, who edited the book, saved me from hundreds of unnecessary commas, weak passive voice verbs, and a myriad other stylistic infelicities. Readers should be as thankful for her as I am.

Others read some or all of earlier versions of the book and offered valuable feedback and encouragement, including Ben Phipps, Tom Parkinson, and Edith Toms. I'm thankful for my faculty colleagues Leanna Fuller, Angela Hancock, Heather Vacek, and Lisa Thompson for encouraging me in my writing and holding me accountable for meeting deadlines. The other member of our faculty writing group, Jannie Swart, died suddenly before the book's completion, and he is dearly missed.

My wife, Ginger Thomas, is always my first reader and my best cheerleader. Thanks, Ginger, for your unfailing love, support, encouragement; for laughing at my jokes; and for the joy you bring to my life. I'm thankful for my children, Simeon, Silas, and Mary Clare, who like having a dad who writes books but wonder when I will write a book that interests them.

I dedicate this book to my mother, Gayle Owens. Thanks, Mom, for the birthday money—and for everything else.

# Introduction

## Give Me Jesus

Saint Augustine was right when he said that our hearts are restless until they rest in God.[1] I know this not because I've been a pastor and a retreat leader who has had the chance to meet a number of restless souls searching here and there for God. I know it because my soul is on its own restless search for satisfaction. And when my soul gets restless, there's only one place it wants to go: the bookstore.

Every year my mother sends me one hundred dollars for my birthday, and every year, when the money arrives in mid-December, I do one thing—drive to the bookstore with the list of books on prayer and spirituality I've been painstakingly revising since Halloween. Buying books calms my anxiety. But buying and reading spiritual books in particular does more than that; it is the way my soul manifests and calms its restlessness. When my own life of prayer is feeling dry, I want to live with God vicariously through the story of someone else's struggle and transformation, searching and finding and searching some more. I crave a new insight or practice that might jump-start my prayer life. I want a book that will make me *feel*. Since my family budget curbs my book-buying throughout the year, by mid-December a year's worth of stored restlessness makes me ready to binge. I will buy books, beg my children and wife to leave me alone, and indulge.

I have become, like so many, a spiritual glutton. When it comes to spiritual gluttony, C. S. Lewis has said that the most dangerous word is "encore."[2] In my spiritual life I always seem to be asking: What's next? And the answer is usually a new book.

Surely this is why God created Christmas vacation—to give me time to read.

It's mid-December and I'm on my way. The book list protrudes from my shirt pocket, and the cash folded in my wallet is begging to be spent. Though I've already ordered two books online, I need immediate gratification, the kind you can only get in a real, as they now say, "bricks-and-mortar" bookstore. I am not paying attention to my driving but daydreaming about sitting in the cozy chair in the corner of the store, a stack of books on the floor next to me. I pick them up one by one, read the cover material and the first few lines of the book, and thumb the pages smelling the book's scent (can't do that online). I'm in heaven.

That's when a voice from heaven spoke to me.

I was daydreaming on Interstate 40 somewhere between Durham and Raleigh, North Carolina, when a voice interrupted my reverie. It wasn't an audible voice. And I have no way of knowing whether it was God's voice, the voice of my own subconscious, or—most likely—both. My college philosophy professor used to ask, "Is it God, or is it gas?" But why do we have to choose between the two? The voice spoke clearly from an unknown depth, and it said, "Let Me be your Teacher"—with a capital M and a capital T. Who else speaks with so many capital letters but God?

That was a word from the Lord that I am still chewing on, not wanting to let it go before I've discovered every implication. One implication showed itself immediately. This word was inviting me to put the brakes on my restless search, to stop reading these kinds of books—at least for a while. Throw away the list, put the money in the bank, and pause. *You are always looking for a new teacher, a new insight, a new way,* the voice seemed to be saying, *but I am the Way, and that is enough. Can you trust that? Everything you need to live life with Me—everything you need to look to Me, receive from Me, and respond to Me with a life of thanksgiving and praise—I myself have already given you. Indeed, I've given you myself. So learn from me.*

This word was calling me to rediscover the simple heart of Christian spirituality—in Jesus, God has given us everything we need. Yes, new practices and insights and disciplines can help us more fully discover what God has given in Jesus, but they can easily distract us. Our searching can actually be an evasion of the simple, though not easy, path of looking at, receiving from, and responding to Jesus.

I wanted to make this rediscovery. The words of the old spiritual were becoming the one song of my own heart: "Give me Jesus."

## JESUS IS ENOUGH

There's another way to state my spiritual condition: I had become a Philip. In John 14, Philip makes a simple request of Jesus: "Lord, show us the Father, and we will be satisfied" (14:8). It might be rude of me to suggest this based on one little request, and I know Jesus himself says not to judge, but Philip's telling Jesus that the disciples will be satisfied if Jesus just shows them the Father makes me think that Philip himself may be a glutton too.

Now, in Philip's defense, we usually associate gluttony—one of the historic so-called seven deadly sins—with food. Most of us think of gluttony as eating too much, the inability to tell when enough is enough at the dinner table. My old ethics professors would put it a little more technically: gluttony is the failure of the virtue of temperateness. The Dominican theologian Herbert McCabe, in his book on the teachings of the Catholic Church, poses the question: "How do we exercise temperateness in the matter of eating and drinking?" And he answers, "We exercise the virtue of temperateness in the matter of eating and drinking by, characteristically, taking and enjoying what is sufficient for our health and for the entertainment of our friends."[3] (I love that he adds "for the entertainment of our friends.") The key word here is *sufficient*. Gluttony, related to food, means habitually taking *more* than is sufficient for the health and entertainment of our friends—an apt description of behavior at most church potlucks.

But the disciples have just eaten supper with Jesus, and nothing in the story suggests that Philip has taken more than is sufficient. Scripture is mum on this point. Philip's gluttony has nothing to do with eating.

Yet other kinds of gluttony tempt us. One of the most pervasive forms of gluttony today is technological gluttony—the marketing-induced belief that suggests this phone, computer, or tablet no longer suffices, and we must have the next iteration hot off the assembly line. In my household we call this phenomenon "iPad Envy."

And if gluttony can relate to food and technology, might it not also relate to spiritual things?

It's laudable to want to see the God whom Jesus called Father. Who wouldn't praise someone for desiring to see God the Father? Shouldn't we all want to? So Philip, who with his request becomes the Patron Saint of All Spiritual Seekers, says, "Jesus, show us the Father, and we will be satisfied."

And I think this request shows his gluttony. I wouldn't think so if not for Jesus' response. Jesus is not satisfied with Philip's desire to be satisfied. You can almost hear the exasperation in Jesus' voice. "Have I been with you all this time, Philip, and you still do not know me? Whoever has seen me has seen the Father. How can you say, 'Show us the Father'? Do you not believe that I am in the Father and the Father is in me?" (John 14:9-10).

Jesus stands right in front of the disciples. He has eaten with them. They've seen him cure diseases and cast out demons and feed thousands, and he's just finished washing their feet. They've also heard him snore at night, seen him get impatient, watched him tire on long journeys. They've seen his frail humanity more fully than anyone.

Jesus in the fullness of his humanity stands before them, and they deem that insufficient. They want more: "Jesus, show us the Father, and we'll be satisfied."

And Jesus responds, if I might paraphrase, "You're stuck with me. But that's okay, because I am enough. I am the Way, the Truth, and the Life. That's all you need."

"Philip," he asks, "can you be satisfied with me?"

And he asks us the same thing. Can we?

## The Way and the Destination

That's what Jesus has been asking me. He interrupted my restless quest for more to ask, "Roger, can you be satisfied with me? Am I enough for you?" It was an invitation to rediscover the heart of Christian spirituality—Jesus.

But what does it mean to say that Jesus is enough?

In the fourth century the church raised similar questions. Questions like these: Who is Jesus, what has he done, and is it enough? The answers weren't clear at the time, and controversies raged as Christian thinkers argued—*fought* might be a better word—over what Christians should believe about Jesus. Two of these thinkers and what they had to say will help us see why Jesus is enough.

The theologian Athanasius (c. 296–373) engaged deeply in a debate about whether the fully human Jesus is fully God as well. Some argued that Jesus is "sort of" divine but not fully. Athanasius effectively defended Jesus' full divinity with a practical argument: If Jesus is not fully divine then he is not enough to get us to our true end as participants in the life of God—the very life Jesus said he came to bring. "I came that they may have life, and have it abundantly" (John 10:10). If he is not God, then how can he bring to us—and bring us to—God's life?

The whole argument of Athanasius can be summarized in one famous phrase: God "assumed humanity that we might become God."[4] Christians call that act of God the Incarnation. God became a human in Jesus so that, through Jesus, we humans may find our true end—our home—in God alone. Jesus, as God, is at once the source of our existence (John 1:3—"all things came into being through him"—is often read at Christmas), the image of our true end as ones transformed through our union with God, and the way to that true end. In his living and dying he brought God's life to us and brought us into God's life.

Jesus—the divine Word who walked among us—is enough. We could say, using Herbert McCabe's words about gluttony to a different purpose—Jesus is more than sufficient. So why look elsewhere?

The other thinker, theologian, and bishop, Augustine (354–430), wrote a small book to help preachers and teachers interpret the Bible. In the process of arguing that the mind of the preacher or teacher requires cleansing by truth, he makes this statement: "Although He is our native country, He made Himself also the Way to that country."[5] God, our native country—a striking metaphor.

If you've ever been in a foreign country, confused by the unfamiliar habits, practices, and speech of that country, you can understand the force of this image. Perhaps you have felt that confusion and homesickness. I certainly felt it as an Indiana native during my fifteen-year sojourn in the South, when I was what Indiana's celebrated poet James Whitcomb Riley called "The Hoosier in Exile."[6] Think of a soldier stationed in a country far from her home. Think of a student taking a junior year abroad. Think of the immigrants to this county who have come hoping for a better life but struggle to imagine how a better life can exist without the language, the songs, the food, and the people that make home home. We internalize the landscapes of our native countries and carry them with us wherever we go. Wherever we are, they call to us.

God, Augustine says, is our native country. From God we came and to God we belong. Our wandering from that native country, our exile, causes the restlessness that Augustine notes, the restlessness that we feel in our bodies and emotions, in our anxieties and our fears, in our yearning for something new, something more. Deep down, it's our yearning to find our way back to our native country.

And that's where Jesus comes in. In Jesus, God—our native country—becomes the way back to our native country. Jesus is the only human being ever to live who never left his native country in God. *Jesus brings God's life to us and us to God's life.*

These sayings of Athanasius and Augustine can be seen as attempts to flesh out for the church Jesus' answer to Philip's question: "Whoever has seen me has seen the Father" (John 14:9). What more than that do we need?

If this train of thought is starting to sound too abstract, if hanging out in the fourth century begins to feel too far from our native country of the twenty-first century, pause and ask yourself: Is there a yearning in me, a restlessness? Maybe you distract yourself from it like I do by shopping for books or some other way—by staying busy or eating ice cream or taking drugs. But isn't it there? Christian spirituality essentially means listening to that restless yearning, hearing it as a yearning to find your way back to your native country in God, and then discovering in Jesus the image of that native country and the way back, all in one.

The word *spiritual* describes a life lived in its native country, God. Jesus called this kind of life "abundant."

## THE SEVEN "GIVENS"

If God says to you, "Let Me be your Teacher," I would not presume to tell you what that means. But I know now what it meant for me. It meant: Stop reading all these books for a while—you use them to fill yourself and avoid me.

17

These words also meant the following: Return to the three practices through which I have been learning to listen to, receive, and respond to Jesus: contemplating the Gospels, praying the Psalms, and sitting with God in silence. These three historic Christian practices form the basis of what I call the "givens" of Christian spirituality. They've been right there from the beginning—no need to search. For a few years the Gospels, the Psalms, and silence had shaped my morning prayer. But in my restlessness and boredom, I began to wander from these practices. They weren't "working" anymore. Time for something new. And God was saying, "Return to these practices. This is the way I will teach you."

After a few more weeks of meditating on the experience I had driving to the bookstore, four other "givens" of Christian spirituality, easy to overlook, became clear to me—the church, the Eucharist, our own bodies, and the poor. These too are ways God has given restless searchers to attend to, receive, and respond to Jesus.

Church. You would think the church would be the first place a pastor would turn. But the church is a messy place. Human relationships get broken, people get angry, feelings get hurt. Ruptures occur. And it becomes easy to forget that this group of people, people I know so well, actually make up the body of Christ. *Really?* Yes.

And Eucharist. When that community gathers to worship and comes to the table where a server says "the body of Christ" and puts a wafer or bread in your hand, it's hard to believe that this "meal" provides a foretaste of our feasting with Jesus when we finally complete the journey to our native country. This bread, this grape juice (alas, I'm a Methodist) in my mouth is the body and blood of Christ for me—the way back to my native country, God.

And our own bodies as well? We can attend to, receive, and respond to Jesus in and through our own bodies? Few Protestants would think this way. For us, Christianity has been an affair of the mind and the heart but seldom our bodies. Yet our bodies drip with water at our baptism, our mouths chew and taste the bread and wine of Communion, our knees bend at the altar rail, our lips form words of praise, and our hands raise in joyful celebration (the latter too rarely for many of us). We don't have to go searching for our bodies. They are here. This frail flesh and bone can aid us in our journey to God.

And, yes, Jesus promises to meet us when we look for him in the "least of these"—the poor, with whom he spent so much time, who were at the heart of his ministry.

The seven "givens" of Christian spirituality—Gospels, Psalms, silence, church, Eucharist, our bodies, and the poor. There are more, but these are enough—what we need to look to Jesus, what we need to receive the life of Jesus, what we need to respond.

This book invites you to journey with me as I tell the story of my own rediscovery of these seven "givens." We'll take some side streets that lead us into scripture and the history of Christianity. You will see signposts along the way—a suggestion that says "Consider This." That gives you a chance to pause, reflect on what you're read-ing, and apply it to your own life. Other signs will say "Try This." If you have the time, do the suggested exercise to practice what we're talking about. Because I suspect you might be reading this book with others—a journey is certainly better with friends—you'll see some signs that say "Discuss This." Use these as conversation starters for group discussion.

I hope by the end of the journey you'll see how Jesus is enough and that what we need to discover and to experience the gracious transformation Jesus has to offer is at hand.

In his poem "The Wild Geese," farmer and writer Wendell Berry describes friends on a Sunday morning horseback ride. They are remembering friends and enjoying the beauty of creation when they see a flock of geese flying overhead. Their abandon in flight is a reminder of what the poet calls faith that "what we need is here." The poem concludes with the hope that we too will choose to live in that ancient faith:

. . . And we pray, not
for new earth or heaven, but to be
quiet in heart, and in eye
clear. What we need is here.[7]

May we gain such clarity about our own faith in God as we journey to our native country. What we need is here.

# 1

## Red Letters and Wild Stories
### *Contemplating the Gospels*

*Let Me be your Teacher.*

    With those words still resonating in my mind, I understand immediately how to begin—with a return to the Gospels and a willingness to rediscover the voice of Jesus through the words and stories that narrate his life and ministry on earth. All those words of Jesus in red letters, so many wild stories—to these we can turn to encounter anew the Teacher. We call these books Gospels because they are ground zero for the good news we find in the words and the life, in the death and the new life of Jesus.

    It's not *the* beginning, though; just a *new* beginning.

    My beginning with the Gospels came a long time ago in a Sunday school room on the second floor of First United Methodist Church, Shelbyville, Indiana, a room partitioned by accordion dividers. Sitting around tables that would be too small for me to sit in now and in wooden chairs that would be perfect for my five-year-old daughter, we kids looked up as our seemingly ancient teacher manipulated flannel figures that adhered magically to a flannel board—angels singing, shepherds watching, wise men bowing, Mary and Joseph bending over a manger with a yellow flannel glow. My introduction to the Gospels began here.

Now I wonder, *Where's the flannel figure of the possessed man in the graveyard, naked, prowling, broken chains dangling from his wrists? Where's the cutout of John the Baptist, not the one where he's preaching in camel's hair but the one after his encounter with King Herod, the flannel cutout with the cutoff head?*

I learned these stories the way so many did, perceiving them as sweet, age-appropriate tales. These stories had not yet found their way into me.

My immature knowledge of the Gospels changed in high school when I started dating a Baptist. I began attending an adult Sunday school class that my girlfriend's dad taught on Sunday evenings. There I saw something I'd never seen before: adults, lots of them, sitting in a room, big leather-bound Bibles flopped open on their laps, earnestly studying. They took notes, asked questions, listened to my girlfriend's father as he taught them the meaning of these stories. Those in the class took these stories seriously, as if their very lives were at stake. Their serious intent was contagious; I wanted to take them seriously as well. So I found in a closet in our house the red Gideon New Testament given to me in the hallway of my elementary school when I was in fourth grade, the only King James Version Bible in the house. Sitting in my bed at night hunched over this little book, the pages sticking together because they'd never been opened before, I read the Gospel of John—the Gospel with the most red letters, page after page of them. I read hoping to discover the power and passion that made those adult Baptists on Sunday nights care so much about these words.

Influenced by these fundamentalist Baptists, I went to a Christian college. But the Bible department at the Christian college I attended was the most open-minded of them all. These professors did not fear alleged contradictions in the Bible, discrepancies between time lines and stories and dates in the Gospels. In one class, studying Matthew, Mark and Luke, the three most similar Gospels, I studied a book called a Gospel parallel, which laid out corresponding stories in the three Gospels in parallel columns. Using different color highlighters, I marked all the similarities and differences. When I finished, the page looked like a rainbow of discrepancies. If in high school I was a thirsty soul reading for my very life, in college I became a scientist methodically dissecting the text.

When I became a pastor, my role as I approached the Gospels changed yet again. Like a server at a soup kitchen I began to read these stories for what I could dish out to others, dipping into them to offer food to hungry pew-sitters on Sunday mornings. Too often I forgot to serve myself. I read these stories for someone else.

I would not change my history with these Gospels. But when my restless soul, no longer filling itself from these now overly familiar stories, started scrambling more and more for the stories of others to fill me, I sensed that the time had come for a new beginning. I needed to adopt what Buddhists call "beginner's mind," and so I read these pages again as if for the first time, sitting at Jesus' feet every day and learning from him.

*Let Me be your Teacher.*

Okay.

Early in this new beginning in the New Year, reading the Gospel of Luke instead of the books I ordered, I encounter Simeon (Luke 2:25-35), and I fall in love with him again. He's old, having waited a long time for "the consolation of Israel" (2:25) without knowing that it would come in this way, carried by two nervous new parents. He's not sure what he's waiting for—like us, so often—but he's waiting in a focused manner. Every day he comes to the Temple prompted by the Holy Spirit. He's eager and expectant and has been for who knows how many years.

I can imagine the scene when Mary and Joseph show up at the Temple with the baby because I remember bringing my first son, named after Simeon, to church when he was one week old. The unsteady, elderly women opened their arms wide hoping to hold the child, and my wife and I nervously handed him over to these grandmothers. I can imagine Mary hesitantly placing Jesus in Simeon's arms. And though he might not have known yesterday what the "consolation of Israel" would look like, he knows today—it looks like a child, about five to six weeks old, fists still clenched, asleep more hours than he's awake. This child is not only the consolation of Israel but the consolation of Simeon as well. He sings a song, and there's nothing generic about it. He doesn't say, "Master, you have now sent a Messiah for your people," but, "Master, now you are dismissing your servant in peace, according to your word; for my eyes have seen your salvation" (Luke 2:29-30). *My* eyes.

To rediscover Jesus at the heart of Christian spirituality, I need to imitate Simeon, to come each day to the Temple of these stories with eager expectancy and no preconceived notions of what I will find or receive, of what will be placed in the arms of my heart. And then, having seen and held and encountered Christ through the red letters and the stories of his life and ministry, I too may be set free, not only for death, as was Simeon, but set free to go into the next moment of my life a little changed, confident that this Jesus goes with me.

## It's All about Jesus

The Bible is often called a book of books, sixty-six in all, more if your Bible has the Apocrypha. So there's a good chance you're asking, Why the Gospels? Aren't all the books of the Bible gifts that can help us hear and respond to God? Why give priority to four?

The answer may seem obvious and noncontroversial: These four are about Jesus. And, while that's the right answer, it needs further exploration.

You can't make sense of Jesus without the rest of the Bible. If Jesus fulfills the law and the prophets (Matt. 5:17), then with no understanding of the law and the prophets (which, together with books called the writings, Christians call the Old Testament), you can't make sense of Jesus.

Yet, after God's self-revelation in the person of Jesus, the earliest Christian thinkers (including the Gospel writers, Paul, and the first theologians of the church) couldn't read the Old Testament without finding Jesus there. Jesus gives Christians a new context. He becomes a lens through which we can see more clearly and understand more fully the reality of God's presence with and work among the people of Israel.

One debate among Bible scholars revolves around how much our knowledge of Jesus affects our reading of the Old Testament. Old Testament scholar Jerome Creach has written a book called *Violence in Scripture*.[1] The book wonders how Christians, living in this age of violence—televised, virtual, and real—make sense of the fact that the Old Testament seems to portray a violent God who wages war, urges people to wage war, and destroys innocent lives.

> CONSIDER THIS
> What is the history of your relationship with the Gospels? How did it start? How has it changed over the years?

It's a complicated question (I'm glad it's Creach's and not mine to answer), but Creach suggests that when scripture contradicts the way of Christ, it's sometimes appropriate for us to seek a symbolic meaning, as Christians have throughout the centuries.[2] For most of Christian history, Christian interpreters of scripture have viewed Christ as scripture's center of gravity.

In a review of *Violence in Scripture*, Walter Brueggemann, a noted Old Testament scholar, objected to the idea of reading the Old Testament from the perspective of Christ.[3] What if, he asks, God really does struggle with violence? By letting Jesus guide our understanding of God in the Old Testament, we make God less complicated than the books of the Old Testament suggest God is.

I cast my lot with Creach. Jesus didn't get himself killed by revealing an uncomplicated God. Reading the Bible and understanding God through Jesus makes God more complicated. Peace is always more complicated and more difficult than violence. The way of Christ won't make your life less complicated, and it won't simplify your understanding of God. The question is whether Christ is the center or not, and if he is, he's the first one we listen to and the last.

DISCUSS THIS

How do you understand the relationship between the Old and New Testaments? What stories have you read in the Old Testament that make you think about Jesus?

One scriptural account reminds me why reading the whole Bible with Jesus in mind makes sense to me. Jesus takes Peter, James, and John up a hill (Mark 9:2-8). And before their eyes he becomes radiant. The disciples shield their eyes but not before they see two others with Jesus—Moses and Elijah, the deliverer of the law and one of Israel's greatest prophets. They symbolize the Jewish Scriptures, the law and the prophets. And they all hear a voice: "This is my Son, the Beloved. . . ." That much had been said before. God said that at Jesus' baptism, "You are my Son, the Beloved; with you I am well pleased" (Mark 1:11). But here, perhaps for emphasis or because some confusion required clearing, God says in the presence of Moses and Elijah, perhaps even speaking to them as well as to us: "This is my Son, the Beloved; listen to *him*!" (Mark 9:7, emphasis added).

Listen to him.

To whom?

To Jesus.

## DEALING WITH DOUBTS AND FEARS

A few days before Christmas I received an e-mail from a reporter writing an article on the challenges of preaching on Christmas Eve. A recent survey had just said that an increasing number of people don't believe the more fantastic stories in the Gospels about the virgin birth, about angels and shepherds and wise men. We live in an increasingly disenchanted world, and these kinds of stories have gone the way of tooth fairies and Easter bunnies. The reporter wanted to know how pastors preached to skeptical people sitting in the pews on Christmas Eve. What advice would I give preachers?

You may be asking yourself a related question: How do I read these stories in the Gospels; how do I listen for the consolation and the challenge Jesus has to offer, when I myself am filled with doubts and skepticism? It's an honest question.

I got the e-mail from the reporter on the first Christmas in eight years that I wasn't preaching. But the question didn't surprise me. For the previous five years I'd preached each week at an urban congregation a mile from a major research university. Deep thinkers, professional skeptics, biblically knowledgeable laypeople, not to mention seminary professors who knew way more than I did packed the pews. A nuclear physicist sang in the choir. The surgeon who performed the state's first liver transplant sat in the back pew. A professor of neuroscience who wrote the definitive book on the effect of drugs on the adolescent brain also sat in the back pew. These people did not approach the Bible with blind trust, with blind *anything*. They were a preacher's greatest challenge, and, I realize now, greatest gift.

> CONSIDER THIS
> When have the miraculous stories of scripture confused or puzzled you? How have you dealt with your confusion?

I faced these folks every Sunday morning. They stood politely when I asked them to stand for the reading of the Gospel. When I said upon finishing, "The Word of God for the people of God," they declared in unison: "Thanks be to God." And I would sometimes think to myself: *Do they stand because I told them to or out of reverence for the Gospel? Do they respond with thanksgiving after the reading because gratitude for these stories wells up in their hearts or because they dutifully read the response printed in the bulletin?*

I suspect that for them and for you—as for me on occasion—it is a combination of both. I am not immune from doubt and skepticism either. I knew that the congregation and I were in this boat together.

Perhaps you have thought about these things. You've moved beyond a kindergarten acceptance; you've read some recent books; and you've begun to ask questions. Some of us fear those first thoughts of doubt that sneak through our minds, as if they indicate betrayal of the people who taught us these stories in the first place. Others of us begin to welcome them as the first signs of liberation from what we are beginning to consider as myths and fables. In either case, we find ourselves wondering: *How do I go on when some of these stories are so unbelievable?*

I would tell you what I have told myself so many times, and what I would tell preachers: "Do not be afraid."

The angel says it often in scripture when he appears to someone: "Do not be afraid" (Matt. 28:5; Luke 1:13, 30; 2:10). He says it to Mary when he shows up to share with her what must have seemed even to her unbelievable news: "Do not be afraid, Mary" (Luke 1:30).

The words *Do not be afraid* spoken to others remind us that we are not alone. We are not the first ones to have doubts and fears. We need not let our fears, doubts, and skepticism alarm us. The church knew from early on that the Gospels told the stories differently, that their sequences and time lines didn't match. Some wanted to take the four Gospels and merge them into one consistent account, but the church said no. We can handle differences and discrepancies; we don't need to reconcile the accounts.

Sometimes we imagine that we are the first people to struggle with the questions. We are not, and that is good news. Do not be afraid, for when we read we find ourselves in a tradition—a community of people who have been reading these stories for almost two thousand years. And the Holy Spirit hasn't stopped using these stories to help people encounter God through Christ, receive God's good gifts, and respond in faith. Why would the Spirit stop now?

For too long the church has been captive to a narrow rationalism. One kind of narrow rationalism, conservative fundamentalism, says, "Believe every word that's written, as it is written, and especially in the King James Version. If we find we can't believe one word, then we can't believe any of it. No doubts allowed. It's all historically true." The other kind, liberal historicism, says, "We can only believe what historians can prove, which isn't much. Build your faith on that." These serve as two sides of the same coin; both doubt God's power.

I suggest that the church has supported a different affirmation: Believe Jesus. Trust this person, who is with us now and who speaks to us through these texts. We come to the scriptures not to build our faith on historically verifiable truths but to encounter a living person, not to worship ink on a page but to worship the living Lord. The testimony of the centuries bears witness that this living Lord uses these words and stories to speak to us, stay in touch with us, and shape our lives—despite our sometimes fleeting, sometimes tenacious doubts.

So, do not be afraid.

I invite you to approach the Gospels with a posture that differs from the one that worries about the stories' credibility. We often unwittingly approach the texts with the posture of the Pharisees and the scribes as so many of the stories depict them—questioning Jesus in order to trap and trick him and catch him with his own words. It's the cynic's posture, and we can easily adopt it when we open these pages.

But we can assume a posture of receptivity. Many of the people in these Gospel stories approached Jesus in just that way. They had less historical knowledge about Jesus than we have. They'd likely never heard of the virgin birth. The broken, paralyzed, shunned—they'd heard rumors that this man could offer them something wonderful: healing, new life. They came to receive, not to question or trick. They came not with a blind trust but with a simple trust—a desire and a longing. They came for a personal, transforming encounter. They came with their hands out.

And we can too.

On Christmas Eve we often sing of Jesus that the "hopes and fears of all the years are met in thee tonight." I would add that doubts—yours and mine—are met in Jesus, and he's not afraid of them. We shouldn't be either. His wide welcome encompasses all we bring.

I don't preach every week anymore, but when I sit in church on Sunday mornings, and the pastor says, "Would you please stand for the reading of the Gospel?" I say with my body: yes. I want to say it with my arms outstretched and my palms open, cupped like a beggar ready to receive.

## GETTING STARTED, NOT FINISHED

I rarely suggest a motto from the tech world as spiritual advice, but I have come to like a Facebook motto: Done Is Better Than Perfect. When it comes to a life of prayer, especially the prayerful reading of scripture, that motto offers useful advice: Don't let needing to get something *right* keep you from doing anything at all.

When we pick up the Gospels to read them with a posture of receptivity, we ask, How? And if you are like me, you will read a book, join a class, attend a workshop; you will want to figure out *how* before you start—so you can get it *right*. Which means, in practice, that you never start at all.

We can change the Facebook motto to fit our purposes: *Started is better than right.* Don't worry about doing it right; just do it. Open those onion-paper-thin pages in your lap, and start to read, slowly, out loud if you want. Maybe say a prayer before you start: "Lord, open my heart so that as I read the stories of your life and the words of your mouth, I can receive whatever you have for me and respond in faith-fulness." Then read. Not too much. It's not a race. We don't want the word *done* in the Facebook motto to throw us off: We are never done. Two verses today is as good as twenty-two if you savor them.

> CONSIDER THIS
> With what attitude do you typically approach the Gospels? Cynicism? Receptivity? Another?

Savor—a good eating metaphor. Food is much more than a bun-dle of nutrients. Eating is a full experience. I know someone once who said if she could get all of her nutrients in a pill, she would be happy never to eat again. But that attitude misses 90 percent of the reason for eating—savoring the food, enjoying the company, and giving thanks for the sustenance of this daily bread. Food involves aroma, texture, taste, flavor, and the conversation that occurs around the table.

My dad used to say, "I'm an advocate of thorough mastication." In other words: chew your food for a long time. Well, I advocate simi-larly when it comes to reading the Gospels—indeed, all of scripture—in order to receive and respond to the One we meet there. Chew thoroughly.

In Christian monasteries over the last fifteen hundred years, a way of reading scripture developed that goes by the Latin name *lec-tio divina*—which means "sacred reading." This approach to reading scripture affirms scripture as more

> CONSIDER THIS
> When have you chosen to read no scripture because you didn't think you could do it "right"?

31

than historical detail, moral advice, or raw material for Christian doctrine. In reading scripture we encounter a person—Jesus. So we read slowly. We reread several times. We linger over words or phrases that stick out to us—that console or challenge us. We pause and ask ourselves, "What is God saying to me through these words that have touched me?"

Four phases make up *lectio divina* as it has been practiced over the many centuries, and these four phases can guide us today. The first phase, *lectio*, means "reading." We begin by reading through the passage slowly and deliberately, simply trying to understand it. The second phase is meditation on the passage (*meditatio*). During this second reading, we chew on the passage. We pay attention to words or phrases that tug at us, and we savor them. I think about my old dog Moe who at Christmas, after he unwrapped his new bone, would disappear for hours to a place where he could gnaw on the bone undisturbed.

The third phase called *oratio*, means "prayer." The entire process of *lectio divina* is prayer. But now, having read and chewed on the passage, hoping to receive everything it has for us, we allow the text itself to lead us into dialogue with God. What do you perceive God is saying to you in this scripture? What do you want to say to God? Have you been consoled, challenged, or some other way moved? Talk to God about it. Talk out loud if you like (no rules here, no right way). Do you need to argue with God, share your doubts or fears with God? Do you identify with one of the characters in the story and need to ask God for healing, understanding, or forgiveness in the same way the character did? Has the passage reminded you of those in your circle for whom you need to pray, even if you don't know why? *Oratio*: let the passage lead you into conversation with God.

And finally comes a phase called *contemplatio*, the Latin word from which we get our rather intimidating word *contemplation*. We'll deal more with this phase in the chapter on silence (see chapter 3), but here let me just say that after all the reading, chewing, and talking, we are being invited to rest in God. Many of us have images of God that prevent us from seeing ourselves as simply resting in God's lap. But eventually words cease, requests run out, arguments stop, and we are invited simply to be with God. Not seeking a feeling. Not looking for an answer. Not actively imagining God, listening to God, or talking to God, but crawling up in the lap of Love, resting our head against Love's breast, and taking comfort in that slow steady heartbeat of grace that says, *This is where you belong.*

*Lectio divina* is tried and true. People throughout the world have practiced it, within monasteries and without, for hundreds of years. But one caveat: it's not a method. So don't become a slave to these phases. If they help you get started, if they open the door a crack to meeting Jesus in the reading of the Gospels, great. But don't get nervous that you are not doing the method "right." The only wrong way to engage this practice is to try to do it right. When I have the pages open in my lap, sometimes the first word or a phrase in the first line will speak to me. That's all I need. I may repeat the word to myself (chewing the bone!) for a few minutes and then rest. No need for words, for active prayer. At other times, I'll read slowly a whole chapter, use my imagination to meditate on the chapter by picturing the people, places, and events of the story. My prayer might be this: "So, God, where do I fit in here?" I might read the same passage for three days. These phases of *lectio divina* are a guide. They give us a key that can open what often feels like a locked door, but each of us will enter the room in a different way.

Don't wait until you've figured it out to walk through the door.

## GETTING UP

January again. I've taken a year to meander through Luke, a year since I've tried to begin again by letting Jesus be my Teacher. And what a year it's been. I live in a different house in a different state, and I have a new job. No longer pastoring a church, now I teach at a seminary. Jesus has guided me throughout. Listening to Jesus through the Gospel of Luke has been indispensable. Sitting in my green La-Z-Boy in the early morning with these pages open in my lap has made me feel like Martha's sister, Mary, in Luke's Gospel. I sit at Jesus' feet, listening and doing the one thing that matters most (Luke 10:42).

This year I'm reading Matthew. I'm in our cold basement (it's Pittsburgh, and this is the year of the much storied "polar vortex") early in the morning before the sun has even thought about coming up. The date: January 3. In today's story the angel warns Joseph to take his family to Egypt where they will be safe from Herod who is hunting for the baby Messiah. "Get up," the angel says, "take the child and his mother, and flee to Egypt" (2:13). And, as I read the whole story, I can't let go of those two words, "Get up."

TRY THIS
Pick a passage from one of the Gospels and spend fifteen minutes with it. Read it slowly. Savor. Pause. Don't worry about doing it right or figuring it out, just read. What do you notice?

I have "gotten up." Six months earlier my family lived in North Carolina, but now we live in Pittsburgh, Pennsylvania. We "got up." I allow my mind to think about how our "getting up" differed from Joseph's and his family's. My family left out of obedience to the voice of vocation, the voice of God's Spirit that says, *This is where you need to be; this is what you need to be doing.* We made the right move, though our lives didn't depend on it in the way it did for Joseph and his family.

But in a way, our lives did depend on it, and I can see my family in this story. The stress and imbalance of our life were crushing us. God used this move to rebalance us. I often prayed the line from a prayer of Thomas Aquinas: "Put my life in good order, O my God."[4] I've been praying that prayer for fifteen years, and I now sense that God is answering it. My family and I got up and embraced a way of life that has more space for God to reorder it, and God is doing just that.

The next day, January 4, I reread the same passage, and the same words, "Get up," strike me again but in another way. Here I am in my basement doing the most important thing—sitting at Jesus' feet, receiving, learning from the Teacher. But the sun is beginning to rise now, and I hear footsteps upstairs. I would like to stay here all day, but I can't.

"Get up," the angel says to Joseph, and we can count on the angel saying that to us every time we open this book. We are called to take this word of scripture—the images, stories, and words of Jesus—into our hearts so that we can respond to them and take them with us into our world, letting them shape our lives in family, community, work, church. Consoled and challenged, we are now compelled to get on with it, knowing that the one we have met through the reading of these pages goes with us.

"Let Me be your Teacher," Jesus says. So we sit. We open the book. We read. And then we get up. Taking what the Teacher has given us, we walk into the light of each new day.

## KEY TAKEAWAYS

In the Gospels God has given us one gift of Christian spirituality, for in the Gospels we can learn directly from the words and stories of Jesus. When we approach the Gospels with an attitude of receptivity, the words and stories of Jesus can shape our relationship with God. If we want to learn from Jesus, then we don't just read the Gospels out of historical curiosity; we read so we can meet a person—Jesus. There's no right way to read the Gospels, but the practice of *lectio divina* can guide us as we seek to savor these stories. Remember this:

- *Do not be afraid.* Don't let fears and doubts keep you from experiencing the Spirit's transformation.

- *Started is better than right.* Don't let not knowing how keep you from opening the Gospels.
- *Get up.* We are meant to live out the good news of the Gospels. Don't stay in your chair; live it.

# 2

# ONE HUNDRED FIFTY PRAYERS
## *Praying the Psalms with Jesus*

Here's how I ended up sitting next to a pool at six-thirty in the morning in McAllen, Texas, just across the border from Reynosa, Mexico, sharing morning devotions with a few others in the high school youth group.

As I mentioned previously, during my junior year in high school I started dating a Baptist, and I had a powerful conversion experience because of the influence of her church (that's a story for another book). A few weeks later, when a deacon announced that the youth would be taking a mission trip to Reynosa, Mexico, to build a church and lead some revival services, this seventeen-year-old, tame Midwestern Methodist boy turned fiery Baptist (until the girlfriend broke up with him) was the first to sign up.

The youth group stayed in a hotel just across the border from Reynosa, crossed into Mexico each day, and came back at night. A few of us—Danny, Daniel, Kelly (the girlfriend), and I—decided we would awaken early to practice our piety by the swimming pool, reading scripture and praying together. No one was swimming at that hour in the morning. We sat at a table with an umbrella. Though the sun was not yet high enough for us to need an umbrella, the heat and humidity made being outside uncomfortable.

We had no plan, but we had our Bibles. I said, "Let's read Psalm 40." I felt surprised even saying this since I'd never read Psalm 40. I'd never read any psalms on my own and was only familiar with the classics from church. I don't know why I suggested this psalm, but the group agreed. We turned to Psalm 40. I started to read aloud out of my new leather King James Bible. God had me within the first three verses:

> I waited patiently for the LORD; and he inclined unto me, and heard my cry. He brought me up also out of an horrible pit, out of the miry clay, and set my feet upon a rock, and established my goings. And he hath put a new song in my mouth, even praise unto our God: many shall see it, and fear, and shall trust in the LORD (Ps. 40:1-3, KJV).

No one had ever told me that I could find my story in the Bible stories, that these stilted Shakespearean sounding words could give voice to the story of my heart. But there it was, my story. This psalm told the story of my recent conversion experience. God lifted me out of the pit of what I now see was high school anxiety, fear, and need for belonging, as much as the pit of sin. God had done something—"love lifted me," as the old hymn goes.

CONSIDER THIS
When has a passage of scripture spoken to you in a clear, personal way? What did you sense God saying?

Until then I had been planning to attend college to study music and singing. Now I had a new song to sing, the song of God's love and forgiveness. It seemed clear at the time: God, through this psalm, was calling me to be a preacher who would sing this new song, so that, like me, others could "see it, and fear, and . . . trust in the LORD."

Two nights later in Reynosa, Mexico, I stood in a cinder-block room with a single lightbulb hanging from the ceiling, a small electric generator powering the light. In front of forty people, mostly the people who lived around the little church we were adding a second story onto, people we had invited an hour earlier when we walked around passing out flyers, I preached for the first time. My sermon went twice the length it should have since each phrase had to be translated into Spanish. I preached about the pit and the God who reached down, lifted me, and offered forgiveness; about the Jesus who went down into the pit of death for us and the God who lifted him up so that we too could have new life. I sang my new song.

Psalm 40 was about me. It was *mine*. The door to the Psalms had been opened and, with it, the door to God, who can speak in and through these ancient prayers.

## OPENING WIDER THE DOOR

For many of us, the door to the Psalms may be cracked open but not any wider. Our relationship with the Psalms might be shallow and episodic at best. In Bible studies that included studying the Psalms, I remember older members reminiscing about how in elementary school they had to memorize Psalms 1; 23; and 100. But the memorization of those psalms marked the boundaries of their knowledge. Others have special relationships for whatever reasons with a few psalms, like my relationship with Psalm 40. Or we might register familiarity with a handful of psalms because of their annual recitation in the seasons of

TRY THIS
Without looking in your Bible, spend ten minutes listing the psalms you know best or phrases from the psalms you remember. What does this exercise tell you about your familiarity with the Psalms?

the church year: Psalm 24 in Advent, Psalm 51 during Lent, Psalm 22 on Good Friday.

When I would plan a funeral with a family, the members would often unreflectively ask that Psalm 23 be read at the funeral, and I would wonder, *Are they asking for this because they've considered their options, and this is their choice or because they don't know enough other psalms—many of which could be equally appropriate to this occasion—to make an informed choice?*

We often can quote verses from the Psalms even if we don't know what psalm they come from: "Be still, and know that I am God!" (46:10). "Make a joyful noise to the LORD, all the earth" (100:1). "Weeping may linger for the night, but joy comes with the morning" (30:5). A few verses tucked in the back pockets of our memories.

The door to the Psalms might be open just a crack. If what we need is here, much of what we need resides in these psalms.

Our limited experience with the Psalms differs significantly from the place the Psalms have held in the life of the church throughout the centuries. Those committed to knowing God and growing in a life with God have found in the Psalms a great resource—the Bible's own prayer book, scripture's very own school of prayer.

Since Christianity began as a Jewish sect and grew out of the first-century Jewish religious matrix, the Psalms were part of early Christianity's DNA. The language of the Psalms was part and parcel of the language of faith, so much so that it's almost impossible to identify all the allusions to the Psalms in the New Testament.

When the Roman Empire became Christian in the fourth century, many Christians moved to the deserts of Egypt, Syria, and Palestine to escape the culturally accommodated Christianity of the empire and to discover and practice a vital faith in the desert. These hermits, known as the desert fathers and mothers, treasured the Psalms. They knew that the Psalms helped them survive not only the austere physical conditions of the actual desert but the spiritual desert in which they learned true growth in prayer. As they sat in their huts, plaiting reeds and making baskets, prayer mainly consisted of reciting the Psalms. They knew the Psalms by heart and said them continuously, thus fulfilling Paul's admonition to "pray without ceasing" (1 Thess. 5:17). Saint David of Wales, the sixth-century patron saint of Wales, influenced as he was by the testimony of the desert monastics, had his monks recite all 150 psalms every day.

As Western monasticism developed and became more communal, with corporate worship and prayer several times a day, the monks chanted the Psalms in worship—as they still do in monasteries around the world—so that they prayed through the entire book of Psalms every week. When we hear the word *meditation*, we often think of yoga or Buddhist mindfulness practices, but for most of Christian history, meditation meant *lectio divina* (discussed in the previous chapter) and praying the Psalms. There was nothing esoteric about it. When the writer of Ephesians enjoins us to speak to one another in "psalms and hymns and spiritual songs" (5:19), the early Christians knew what he meant. The book of Psalms is the Bible's own hymnbook, and we can't be too familiar with all its hymns.

These monks might ask why we come so rarely to this book when God, through the poets of God's people Israel, has laid out for us a banquet that will never spoil? Indeed, why do we pick and choose so sparingly (like my children at a Chinese buffet), when we could come and be satisfied? Why do we search aimlessly here and there, high and low, for spiritual nourishment, when before us we have the prayers that have taught, shaped, and sustained Jews and Christians for centuries? God says in Psalm 81, "Open your mouth wide and I will fill it" (v. 10). Why not let God do this through the Psalms?

What did these early Christians know that we have forgotten? They knew—and we can rediscover—what reformer Martin Luther said about the book of Psalms: "In it is comprehended most beautifully and briefly everything that is in the entire Bible."[1]

In our restless search, looking for something to satisfy when our common experiences grow boring, we may not notice that God has prepared a table before us, a banquet, at which our cup will run over. When we open the door all the way and walk into this banquet hall of prayer called the Psalms, where Jesus welcomes and teaches us around the table, we can say with the writer of Psalm 63: "My soul is satisfied as with a rich feast, and my mouth praises you with joyful lips" (v. 5).

## PRAYING THE PSALMS WITH JESUS

The Psalms are the prayers of God's people, the Jews. And Christians, from the beginning, have seen in the Psalms signposts pointing to the life of Jesus. The Gospel writers refer to the Psalms often to make sense of Jesus' own life, and today we use the Psalms throughout the church year to point us to events in his life. Jesus himself, hanging on the cross, cried out the words of Psalm 22, "My God, my God, why have you forsaken me?" (v. 1), and ever since Christians have seen in the Psalms intimations of Jesus' life. When I sing to my daughter before bed, "The King of Love My Shepherd Is," I'm using a song based on Psalm 23 to tell her about Jesus, who, as she already knows, is the shepherd of Psalm 23. The Psalms point forward to Jesus; Jesus fulfills the Psalms. Through the Psalms, Jesus can be our Teacher.

Perhaps more than any other person, the twentieth-century German theologian and martyr Dietrich Bonhoeffer, hanged by the Nazis, helped us realize the profound connection to Jesus available through the Psalms. When we pray the Psalms we not only say prayers that point to Jesus' life but also say the prayer *of* Jesus; in praying the Psalms we become joined to the one great prayer that is Jesus himself.

Throughout Adolf Hitler's reign as chancellor of Germany, Bonhoeffer opposed Germany's anti-Jewish laws. When Hitler declared the church of Germany to be the state church, Bonhoeffer helped form the Confessing Church, a church that opposed the accommodated, national church. Though illegal, the Confessing Church continued to train pastors. Bonhoeffer himself ran an illegal, underground seminary for several years before the Gestapo closed it. After the seminary was closed, Bonhoeffer wrote his classic book *Life Together*, which gives an account of the kind of Christian community the seminarians shared. It also paints a picture of what true Christian community can look like in order to witness to God's faithfulness in an increasingly unbelieving world.[2]

Daily prayer lay at the heart of this Christian community's life together, which began every morning with the Psalms. Bonhoeffer says that the Psalms occupy a unique place in the Bible because they are at once scripture—God's word to us—and at the same time human prayers addressed to God. "How," he asks, "can God's Word be at the same time prayer to God?"[3] Bonhoeffer answers his own question:

> The *human* Jesus Christ to whom no affliction, no illness, no suffering is unknown, and who yet was the wholly innocent and righteous one, is praying in the Psalter through the mouth of his congregation. . . . Because Christ prays the prayer of the Psalms with the individual and with the church before the heavenly throne of God, or rather, because those who pray the Psalms are joining in the prayer of Jesus Christ, their prayer reaches the ears of God. Christ has become their intercessor.[4]

Bonhoeffer gives us an almost mystical insight into what happens when individuals and the church take the Psalms onto their lips. Because the church is Christ's body and Christians through baptism are joined to Christ, when we pray the Psalms—the very prayers Jesus would have known and prayed by heart when he walked the earth— we continue to offer his prayers with our voices. When the church prays the Psalms and individual members of it pray, Jesus himself is praying in and through us, according to Bonhoeffer.

This truth was highly significant for the Confessing Church in their struggle with Nazi anti-Semitism. When they prayed the Psalms, these Jewish prayers, they joined their voices with the voice of Jesus.

For these pastors-in-training, praying the Psalms became an act of resistance.

Bonhoeffer's insight that we encounter Jesus and participate in the prayer of Jesus when we pray the Psalms helps us in a practical way. Perhaps you've experienced reciting a psalm in church and thinking these thoughts: *This psalm has nothing to do with me.* Perhaps in the psalm an innocent victim is pleading to be rescued from enemies, or a wounded soul cries out to God in despair, and you think *I'm not going through this. How can I pray this?*

Bonhoeffer recognized this problem. He states that when we start praying the Psalms, we're bound to find some that don't match our experience. They seem foreign; they feel awkward on our lips, which may explain our selective relationship with the Psalms—we are accustomed to praying only the ones that sync with our personal experience. But many—the psalms of vengeance or despair or even praise—seem ill-suited to our voices. Do we simply skip them?

No, because these psalms are not only our individual prayers; as the prayers of Christ, they are the prayers of the church. And someplace, someone with whom we are united through Christ, is suffering what this psalm expresses. So we can legitimately pray them on behalf of the innocent, angry, joyful, or despairing people throughout the world. We don't have to feel the emotions that each psalm expresses in order to pray it because we pray as ones joined to Christ. In practice this means that when we encounter a psalm in our private prayers or in corporate worship that mismatches our experience, we can offer the prayer in solidarity with people we know or ones unknown to us for whom this prayer is just right. All this is possible through our union with Christ.[5]

In praying the Psalms, we do not just hear and respond to Jesus by letting him be our Teacher in the school of prayer called the Psalms—though we are doing that. We participate in the prayer that is Jesus' own life, his offering himself to God in word and deed, prayer and sacrifice, for the whole world.

## Embrace Your Curiosity

What is it about a door that's ajar that makes us want to open it and peek inside? Especially if the door has a Do Not Enter sign on it.

For my son Silas's ninth birthday, my wife and I rented a gym at a neighborhood community center so he and his friends could play basketball together. The kids brought their own balls, but the woman who worked for the community center thought we might want some more. So while we were eating birthday cake, she went into a room off the gym overflowing with sports equipment and picked four extra basketballs for us. However, she failed to close the door all the way. She didn't know it, but she was breaking the spirit of the Lord's Prayer by leading a bunch of nine-year-olds into temptation.

I don't think they would have expressed interest in the door if the staff person had only left it open. But a sign dangled next to it: Keep Door Closed at All Times—Community Center Staff Only. A clear invitation to transgression! I noticed the boys gathering in the corner of the gym near the slightly open door, so I walked over. And they could see through the crack the many colors of sports equipment piled around—blue mats, red balls, yellow nets, orange cones. What kid wouldn't want to pull each piece of equipment out and play with it? Why be stuck with only basketballs? But one kid, the youngest one and a clear rule follower, walked up to me and said, "I think we should close that door; just read the sign." "You can close it," I said. He did, and that ended the temptation.

It's as if the Psalms have a door. Maybe the door to the Psalms has been cracked open for you, the way Psalm 40 cracked the door open for me. Perhaps this chapter has piqued your interest and inspired you to look around the edge of the door to see what various treasures the room holds. And yet we hesitate. We sense a sign on the door: Experts Only. We know that some songs and poems in this room are too hot for us to handle. The psalms of vengeance, for example. How can we touch those? Better shut the door for our safety.

Or maybe it's not the psalms of vengeance that scare us; maybe the psalms that suggest deep intimacy with God make us afraid. "As a deer longs for flowing streams, so my soul longs for you, O God" (Ps. 42:1). Though we may acknowledge such longing deep down, the kind of longing that can fuel a restless search for spirituality, we also perceive the danger of being so close to God, being one of God's intimates. A transforming relationship with God, though what we all long for, can upset the applecarts of our lives. Maybe we can hold that intimacy at bay. Shut the door.

My word to you is this: Let the longing win; embrace the curiosity. These treasures belong to more than the brave, the holy, the few. They belong to you; they give voice to your longing, fear, anxiety, loneliness, and hope. This is a storehouse of discovery—a book of prayer that can help you discover yourself and a faithful God. Open wide the door and see what's inside.

I know the Psalms can intimidate so I want to suggest two ways of entering this book that can help you realize that these prayers—the ancient prayers of the Jewish people, the prayers of Christ, and the prayers of the church—are your prayers too.

Practice putting a psalm into your own words. The Psalms truly express the whole range of human emotion and experience, the ones that society deems okay and the ones we are told are shameful and taboo, like the cries of hatred and calls for vengeance. Yet, as human beings, we feel these emotions sometimes; we would be lying if we said we didn't. But we don't always know how to put our feelings into words of prayer or even wonder if it's okay to do so. And some feel as uncomfortable talking about longing for an intimate relationship with God as denouncing enemies. In either case, the Psalms can help. A psalm can tutor us in prayer.

The practice is simple. Take a psalm that you believe expresses your prayer, one that resonates with you for whatever reason. Scientists talk about "limbic resonance" as a way to name how animals can sense the emotional state of another animal. I believe the Psalms embody "soulful resonance." Our souls may resonate with a psalm in a deep way, even if we can't say why. Read the psalm aloud. And then, with pen in hand, rewrite the psalm in your own words, using the psalm's structure as a guide.

TRY THIS
Take Psalm 40; 42; 63; or 65 and rewrite it in your own words. How can this practice help you pray?

Take Psalm 42:1 for example: "As a deer longs for flowing streams, so my soul longs for you, O God." How would you express this psalm's prayerful sentiment in your own words? Only you know how you would do it, but I might write something like this: "God, I want to know you, to have a full and deep relationship with you because you are like water—the very source of life. The source of my life." There is no right way to do this. If you are studying this book with a group, and group members decide to share what they've written, it's important that everyone realizes no one is competing. Members will use this exercise as a way of sharing with one another their lives of prayer.

But what about enemies? When I encounter psalms that ask for deliverance from enemies, I look at my life to see what, if anything, feels like an enemy. I don't often have flesh-and-blood enemies, so I struggle to imagine people I need to be delivered from. (Okay, it's easier than you might think.) But I can recall times when I struggled with severe anxiety that felt like an

DISCUSS THIS
Ask group members to rewrite one of the four psalms mentioned above and then share with the group. If everyone chooses the same psalm, it will be interesting to see the differences.

enemy. When I would read one of those psalms, I substituted anxiety for enemy, and the psalm became a perfect expression of my inner anguish. If you find a verse that simply doesn't fit, skip it. Remember: no rules here.

Eventually you will discover two things. First: You no longer need pen and paper; you can say the prayer or imagine how this prayer could be yours by saying inwardly the words that the psalm inspires in you. And second: You may find that the psalm becomes a prompt for your own prayer. It gets you started, and you discover that you are no longer paraphrasing the psalm but writing or saying your own prayer, revealing a desire for God's action in your life in a way that surprises you. And with that discovery, the door to the Psalms opens a touch wider.

This practice alone can remain shallow and episodic if you find the five psalms that "work" for you and ignore the rest. For that reason, along with the personal appropriation of the Psalms, I suggest a recovery of the practice of praying the Psalms in order regularly. Pray through all one hundred and fifty and let them challenge, confound, and, ultimately, form you over time.

You can tackle this in a number of ways. The Episcopal Book of Common Prayer (BCP) arranges the Psalms for use in morning and evening prayer. If you prayed according to the schedule in the BCP, you'd get through all one hundred and fifty every month. Old Saint David of Wales, who prayed all one hundred and fifty each day, might accuse you of weakness, but the adage of John Chapman—"Pray as you can, and do not try to pray as you can't"—applies here.[6] Trying to pray all one hundred and fifty in a day or even a week will be for most of us a way we *can't*. So don't even try.

CONSIDER THIS
How could you incorporate praying through the Psalms in your life? What way would work best for you?

When I tried to use the BCP, I learned that praying all the Psalms in one month counts as a way I can't. With my desire to linger in the

Gospels and my need for extended silence in prayer, I acknowledged that I simply couldn't pray that many psalms every morning and evening. So I improvised. I took my Bible, opened to the Psalms, and made my own divisions. In my Bible, if you looked, you would find a code that lets me know whether a Psalm is to be read in the morning or the evening, and on what day of even and odd numbered months. My divisions get me through all the Psalms in order, prayed morning and evening, over a two-month period. Saint David might be thinking I'm lax, but this approach works for me. Your job is not to do what works for me, Saint David, or Episcopalians but what works for you. One psalm a day? All of them twice a year? Experiment, then adjust until you find what fits.

Regularly reading through the Psalms in order—and you decide what is regular for you—will vastly improve your ability to do the first practice, to find the psalm that resonates with you when you need it and use it to guide your prayer. Each month I marvel at the way a psalm will strike me, either one I've never given a second thought to or one that's so familiar I never believed I could hear it afresh.

This way of reading the Psalms is both deep and wide. It opens the door all the way. Only by experience will you truly discover: No sign out front says Keep Out. After a while, you'll know your way around this room, and you'll be familiar with its treasures. You'll be glad you entered.

## STILL SINGING A NEW SONG

Now, in the morning on the fifteenth day of odd-numbered months, I read Psalm 40—the one I read for the first time next to a swimming pool in Texas. It's an old friend by now. And as with old friends, our relationship has changed over the years. But it still reminds me of that one, unforgettable moment when I felt called to be a preacher.

I'm not a preacher anymore, at least not every week. I'm not the pastor of a church. I teach in a seminary and only preach when invited. But this change does not indicate a denial of my call because over the years the meaning of this psalm, through my returning to it again and again, has deepened. Now, when I read that God has put a "new song in my mouth," I don't see this narrowly defined as the task of preaching. That new song is my whole life; whatever I'm doing, my whole life is a song of praise to God—or at least I want it to serve that way.

Sometimes I sing that song from the pulpit—but I also sing it to Mary Clare, my five-year-old, before she goes to sleep. I sing it to my wife, as I listen to her tell me about a restful day or when I'm welcoming a visitor to the church where I worship. I sing it when I'm sitting at a computer, like I am now, struggling for words that might help others sing the songs of their own lives. The song is nothing other than my vocation to be me. "For me to be a saint means to be myself," wrote Thomas Merton.[7] This is what Jesus has been teaching me through this psalm and others over the past twenty years—but mostly since I started walking daily into this room of psalms and learning to live in it.

Every two months I can count on seeing Psalm 40, my old friend. And who knows how our conversation will change over the years?

## Key Takeaways

We may be unfamiliar with the Psalms because they seem strange and address subjects like vengeance and hating enemies that make us uncomfortable. But when we discover that in the Psalms we join in Christ's prayer and pray in solidarity with others, the door to the Psalms can open wider for us to step in. Two practices can help us incorporate the Psalms into our lives. We can practice putting a psalm into our own words, and we can find a way to pray regularly through all one hundred fifty psalms. Remember this:

- *There is no right way.* When you put a psalm into your own words, don't worry about what others might think. There is no right way to do this.
- *Christ is at the center.* When you come to a psalm that doesn't express your feelings, keep in mind that through your union with Jesus you are praying in solidarity with others who are experiencing the circumstances of this psalm.
- *Exploration is encouraged.* Dive into the psalms anywhere. Go exploring. Don't be intimidated, and see what happens!

# 3

# THE QUIET CENTER
*Learning to Befriend Silence*

I call it the paradox of silence: We want silence, and we flee it. No one had to tell me about this paradox. I found it on my own.

My wife, Ginger, was attending a weeklong spiritual formation retreat. I was a busy pastor left at home with two even busier toddler boys. My only goal each day, besides survive, was to get the boys in bed early and enjoy a quiet evening. One night that week I had to put the older boy back in bed more than forty times. Quiet eluded me.

One evening, though, I managed—after the boys finally fell asleep and after cleaning up the kitchen and getting the next day's to-do list in good order—to plop down in the green La-Z-Boy (the one you've already met, the same one I read and pray in today) to taste a moment of quiet while I struggled to keep my eyes open. That night I began reading an old, used, yellowing-paged copy of Thomas Merton's book *Contemplative Prayer*. I have no idea where I got this book; I have come to believe providence put it in my hand. I'd never read a book by Merton before but was aware of his stature as the great twentieth-century contemplative monk and teacher of prayer.

The book begins with this warning: "What is written about prayer in these pages is written primarily for monks." But he affirms that other Christians should "be able to read and make use of what is here said for monks, adapting it to the circumstances of their own" lives.[1] I hoped so, knowing that no life could be further from a monastic one than mine. The book offered a vision of prayer that appealed to me. Merton spoke a language my own soul understood. I hoped even more that the kind of prayer he spoke about—the stillness the monks sought—might be possible for a busy pastor-dad trying to finish a PhD, visit the sick, preach decent sermons, and pay at least minimal attention to his family. I feared not.

DISCUSS THIS
Why do you think so many people today hunger for silence and solitude?

So captivated by what I was reading, I forced myself to read on despite my fatigue when I came to Merton's discussion of the relationship between "activity" and "contemplation" in the Christian life. One passage in particular struck me. Merton describes two very active leaders and preachers in history—one a pope, the other a busy abbot—and says that by looking at their lives, "we can sense that their contemplative experience is somehow deeper and richer" because of the grace God gave them to "preach to others."[2]

I had to stop, back up, and read that again.

Merton knows of people in the "active life"—which I took to be people like me—who are as deeply contemplative as the habit-clad, silence-loving, life-infused-with-prayer monks he lives with.

That passage awakened in me the possibility that a silence I'd never known but longed for might be possible for me. I had no cloister, no abbot, no bell ringing seven times a day to remind me to turn my heart toward God, no chanting of the Psalms in worship, no spiritual reading during silent meals, no hours alone meditating on scripture in my room—none of that. And yet, if he knows of contemplative active-life people, knows they have existed, *maybe*, I thought, *I could be one*. Maybe I could drink from the chalice of silence.

Here's what happened (I later learned it happens to almost everyone and will happen to you): When I tried to enter the silence by repeating a prayer word, a mantra—images, thoughts, and fears flooded my mind. Because a few years earlier I'd been mugged while in my car, a mugging that involved a gun, a bang, broken glass, blood, and my thinking that I'd been shot. The images that came to me in the silence were frightening. The trauma of that mugging seemed to have wired a new circuit in my brain through which the images of this event looped as well as any like them that I have seen since. My subconscious attempted to hold them at bay by keeping busy: reading, singing, cleaning, thinking, coping.

But as soon as I sat and tried to be still, this Pandora's box opened. We all have a Pandora's box that can open when we sit down and turn off the noise. For some, the thoughts are dark and frightening. For others, they are deadly dull. We may despair in the silence, not about the macabre contents of our subconscious but about how boring our lives are.

Silence: As much as I longed for it, I learned to avoid it.

I don't know anyone who has described this paradox more clearly than Henri Nouwen: "As soon as we are alone, without people to talk with, books to read, TV to watch, or phone calls to make, an inner chaos opens up in us. This chaos can be so disturbing and so confusing that we can hardly wait to get busy again. . . . When we have removed our outer distractions, we often find that our inner distractions manifest themselves to us in full force."[3]

CONSIDER THIS

When you try to be silent, what goes on in your mind? What emotional responses do the things you imagine trigger in you? Fright? Boredom? Excitement?

Is there a way to answer our longing for silence and avoid the risk of inner chaos?

## WHY SILENCE?

Before we ask, "Is there a way?" we should consider a more basic question: "Why would we want to?" If facing our inner chaos is the fruit of stillness, why not just stay busy?

At a recent retreat, I delivered a talk about the practice of silence. With eloquence, wisdom, and wit (I imagined) I explored the practice of silence, its whys and its hows, so that those gathered might receive more fully this Christian "given." At the end of the presentation, before I dismissed the retreat participants to go into an hour of silent prayer, one person raised his hand. He had a simple question: "Could you state in one sentence what the purpose of silence is?" So much for eloquence and wisdom. At least I can still imagine my wittiness.

One reason we would choose to go into the silence is that Jesus habitually sought solitude and silence. At the beginning of his ministry, he spent forty days in the wilderness where even he confronted the dark side of silence. "He was in the wilderness forty days, tempted by Satan" (Mark 1:13). Jesus didn't let the paradox of silence deter him from its formative necessity in his life before he began his ministry. And such withdrawal seems to be a pattern in his ministry. "In the morning, while it was still very dark, he got up and went out to a deserted place, and there he prayed" (Mark 1:35). Christians throughout the centuries—hermits who lived alone in the desert and spent their days in silence, monks who lived in communities but spent hours each day in silence, mystics who enjoyed being with God in meditation and contemplation—have looked to the practice of Jesus himself. They found in Jesus' habit of silent communion with God a model for their own.

But these early practitioners also began to articulate a theology of silence. In prayerful silence, the desert fathers and mothers said we confront temptation and inner chaos and we learn how to deal with both our frightening and boring thoughts so that we can come to taste stillness. Stillness comes from the Greek word *hesychia*, a term that named an inner tranquility that made possible a life of availability and openness to God. At the beginning of our practice of silence, we realize that with all our thoughts, temptations, and distractions, a great deal of white noise interferes with our ability to be open and available to God. The practice of silence, of learning to handle thoughts, fears, and distractions, leads us to a place of deep openness, an openness that allows us to receive and respond to Jesus.

Christian mystics, like Meister Eckhart and Teresa of Avila, among others, took this a step further. They believed that in contemplative silence we could discover that God lives at the foundation of our very souls, in the depths of our being. We already have union with God. The practice of contemplative silence leads us to the place where we can realize this union. Silence helps us discover our union with God and allows our union with God to form our living.

Given the history of the Christian practice of contemplative silence, it's important to pay attention to the fact that the practice of silence is, at its heart, a receptive practice, a practice of making us open and available to receive the presence and action of God within us.

Often because of our language of spiritual "practices" and "disciplines," we think these practices of prayer, even silence, are things we *do*. They sound effortful, perhaps a way we can advance our projects of self-improvement or ways we can thrust ourselves along the journey of holiness. *I'm doing it*, we think. *This is my action.*

CONSIDER THIS
How do you think of spiritual disciplines? Do you consider them exercises *you* do or ways to open yourself to what God does?

57

Ruth Burrows, an English nun who has written extensively on prayer and the spiritual life, corrects our thinking on this matter:

> On our side prayer is simply being there: open, exposed, inviting God to do all God wants. Prayer is not our activity, our getting in touch with God, our coming to grips with or making ourselves desirable to God. We can do none of these things, nor do we need to, for God is there ready to do everything for us, loving us unconditionally. . . .
>
> Our whole concern in whatever we do must have as its aim to hold us 'there' in faith before God. . . . We must bear in mind that all we are trying to do is to help ourselves to be present for God to love us.[4]

In silence we are present with God, who is the very heart of our heart, present with us, loving us from the inside out.

We can try to define what we do and what God does in the silence, and how it relates. But I prefer pictures. This morning my five-year-old daughter gave me a picture. I was praying, practicing silence, and she awakened earlier than usual. Almost silently she scooted on her bottom down the stairs and walked over to where I was sitting. I lifted her into my lap, where she curled up, putting her head against my chest. She didn't ask for anything or say anything. She just lay her head on my chest where, I imagine, she could hear my heartbeat. I thought of the beloved disciple in John's Gospel at the Last Supper, "leaning on Jesus' bosom," as the King James Version translates it (John 13:23).

That's what we do in silence—lean against God's breast, listening to the heartbeat of love for us that is closer to us than our own heartbeats and that outlasts our own heartbeats and that is steadier than our own heartbeats.

After the participant in the retreat humbled me by asking such a simple question at the end of my hour-long monologue on silence, I paused, and said, "In silence we can rest in our fundamental union with God." I can't state it more simply than that. But in my mind I pictured the beloved disciple resting on Jesus' bosom, receiving the gift of Jesus' presence. And now I imagine my own little girl in my lap, resting her head on my chest. We rest in the God who rests in our souls.

## OBSTACLES TO SILENCE

But having some ideas about what silence is or why we might practice it—even having a longing for silence fueled by a deeper understanding of the "what" and "why" of silence—doesn't remove the obstacles. Whenever I teach on silence, I ask what makes the practice of silence difficult. You will not be surprised that "distracting thoughts" usually tops the list. But let's deal with others first, before we come back to that one.

Our external conditions can present an obstacle to silence. Our mornings are rushed. We work all day. We veg in front of the TV or surf the web to wind down at night. Then we fall into bed. In between we do everything else we need to do, and there is no time left. When are we just going to sit for ten, fifteen, or twenty minutes?

TRY THIS
Write a list titled, "My Life Conditions That Prevent Silence." What on the list seems easiest to change?

On top of that, the house is a mess, and there is no comfortable place to embody a peaceful, calm presence.

The silence we are talking about cannot be reduced to external silence alone, but external silence and some order are often preconditions for the inner stillness we seek.

When a noisy, disordered life blocks the way to silence, the only question is this: How badly do you want it? How desperately does your soul long to rest in God? How acutely do you desire the heartbeat of God's love to beat in and through you? As Quaker Thomas R. Kelly writes, "If you say you haven't the time to go down into the recreating silences, I can only say to you, 'Then you don't *really* want to.'"[5]

The best wisdom says you address this obstacle by establishing a "when" and a "where." Without these, the practice will be nearly impossible. Can you put on your calendar twenty minutes at the beginning of your day—which could involve getting up a little earlier or going to bed a little earlier (which for most of us is not a bad idea)? Can you create a little order near one comfortable chair, put some flowers on a nearby table, and light a candle? You will be surprised how a simple, inviting space can call you into silence when a physically chaotic space, a space that mirrors the chaos of your soul, makes you want to run.

CONSIDER THIS

If you had to pick a "when" and a "where" right now, what would they be? What would you have to change to make them work?

Another obstacle: "I just can't do silence! Silence is not me!"

Recently I taught a seminary course in spirituality. We discussed and practiced silence together. I required the students to keep a journal in which they reflected on how the practice was going and to turn their journal entries in to me weekly. June, in her fifties, is a second career student-pastor. Early in her journal entries she wrote, "I'm scared of silence. My mind is too busy. I can't sit still. I don't do silence." She wrote about how impossible she knew this would be and that she feared wasting her time.

As the weeks went by, her journal entries changed. She began to write things like, "I've sat for ten minutes in silence each morning this week. I can't believe it." Then later: "Fifteen minutes! I'm beginning to wonder what I would do without the silence."

At the end of the term, she sent me an e-mail:

Dr. Owens, I have enjoyed this class tremendously and hope that I will be able to take another one of your classes in the future. I wanted to tell you that I am still practicing silence. It is becoming part of the rhythm of my life. For this I am most thankful and will always remember this class and you as the inspiration for bringing this precious part of my spiritual journey. Thanks for everything.[6]

Some people may be constitutionally unable to sit in silence, but most people need to hear that if June can do it, they can do it.

I've known the unlikeliest candidates who have managed to practice silence: folks suffering from post-traumatic stress, people plagued with chronic anxiety, restless souls fidgeting because of attention deficit disorder. If they can do it, I'm guessing you can too. At least it's worth a try.

## THE FOUR RS OF PRACTICING SILENCE

But that first obstacle will make you want to quit if you start: Distractions, the obstacle at the heart of the silence paradox—the thoughts, feelings, emotions, fears, and anxieties that inhabit the chaotic landscape of our minds. We sit in silence, and we can't stand it. We have to run away. What do we do? At this point, methods for silent prayer come into play, for most address this particular situation—what Buddhists call "monkey mind" and what Martin Laird calls "the wild hawk of the mind."[7]

There is not one Christian way of practicing silence. There's a family of ways, and while significant family resemblances exist, so do differences. Different trajectories in history, grounded in different theologies, written in different eras—though consonant with one another. And different practitioners of the twentieth and twenty-first centuries have tried to package the wisdom of these Christian traditions for contemporary seekers.[8]

What follows is my own take on one member of the broader family. It is not the *right* way or the *only* way but one I have found most helpful and easy to explain. It has helped me live through and continue to live in the paradox of silence without running away. It has guided me to a sense of approaching rest in God. Close enough that I can almost hear God's heartbeat. I offer it with the hope that it will help you as well.

The way of silence that has influenced me is the way that involves choosing a prayer word, a short word of significance to you that expresses or symbolizes your desire to be with God. The word I use is *Jesus*. Obviously, the name Jesus has a long history in Christian contemplative practice. The tradition of saying the Jesus Prayer—"Lord Jesus Christ, Son of God, have mercy on me, a sinner"—has had a storied history especially in Eastern Orthodox prayer, and many simplify that prayer to the name Jesus, the name of the One who makes our praying possible. But there are other options: *shalom, Abba, peace*. Don't get hung up on choosing the right word. There isn't a right word. Pick one and stick with it.

And then, sitting comfortably in the silence, slowly repeat the word to yourself, half of the word on the in-breath, half on the out-breath. Give this word your attention as best you can. Without trying too hard, simply pay attention to the word as you say it silently in your mind.

Now, I know what you're thinking about me when I describe this method: *This is what you tried, and this is where the images and thoughts began to drive you crazy. This is how you discovered the paradox. I thought you already failed doing this!*

But that was before I knew the heart of the practice, what I have come to call (in stereotypical preacherly alliteration), the four *R*s of contemplative silence: Repeat, Recognize, Release, and Return. When you grasp the work of these four movements, you will begin to open the gift of silence.

*R* number one: *Repeat.* Silently and slowly repeat the word to yourself, as I suggested above.

And then *R* number two: *Recognize.* Soon after you start saying your prayer word, your mind will wander. *Enter distracting thoughts stage left.* The content of these thoughts does not matter, whether of your happiest birthday party as a child, an exam you have to take tomorrow, or a traumatic event in your past. This practice helps us to stop judging our thoughts and start noticing when we have them. You notice—you recognize that you are thinking. You are engaged in internal dialogue; you are imagining a mental picture; you are caught up in a fantasy of revenge. You are thinking.

Most of the time our minds are working—thinking, dreaming, imagining. The practice of silence gives us the chance to recognize this. We simply wake up to the fact that we are no longer focusing our attention on a prayer word, and we are caught up in a thought. Our attention has been stolen; we are distracted.

You've had this experience: You're driving to the grocery store, and about a half a mile past the store you wake up to the reality that you got so caught up in your thoughts you didn't notice passing the store. You recognize this. This second movement of the practice invites us to do that—recognize. You repeat to yourself the prayer word and then notice—recognize—when your mind wanders from the word into a more attractive or fearful thought.

This is the point when we *release*, *R* number three. We let go. A shiny thought has floated across our awareness, and the tendrils of our mind have reached out to grab it. We recognize this occurrence, acknowledge our lack of attention to the repetition of the word, and we let go. We release the thought. We don't fight the thought. We don't judge the thought. We don't say to ourselves, *You idiot, look, you are thinking instead of focusing on the prayer word.* But if we do say that to ourselves, that's just another thought we get to release.

Q: But how do we release a thought—that's the whole problem!

A: The fourth *R—Return.*

We release by returning to the repetition of the prayer word. We were repeating a prayer word; we were giving it our complete attention. Then an interesting thought floated across the horizon of our awareness and snagged our attention. So we left the repetition of the word in order to think the thought, to engage in this act of imagination or internal dialogue or scheming and plotting or *whatever the thought was about*. And then we woke up; we recognized our thinking, that our "wild hawk of the mind" was off doing frantic circles in the sky of our imagination. So now, we release the thought gently (without commentary and additional thinking) and return to our repetition of the word.

At first, this can feel like moving through four separate steps, awkward and clunky. But because our minds are so frequently distracted, we get plenty of practice. After a while it becomes one almost unnoticeable movement.

Resting in our union with God, discovering that "it is no longer I who live, but it is Christ who lives in me" (Gal. 2:20), is a lifelong journey of letting go of our own agendas, images, and fantasies so we can live in constant communion with the Christ living in us. The practice of silence is a microcosm of that lifelong process. Every day, for twenty or thirty minutes, we can practice dying to the attractions and aversions that compel us so that we can, as we were meant to do and as we will throughout eternity, rest in God.

## DESCENDING INTO THE SILENCE

Henry David Thoreau said, "I should not talk so much about myself if there were anybody else whom I knew as well."[9] I want to put some flesh on this theory by painting a picture of what the silence can look like in practice. And because I know myself better than I know anyone else, the picture has to be of me. It's a picture some nine years after my first exhausted and fearful late-night encounter with the paradox of silence, a picture of what's possible.

Quaker Thomas Kelly talks about going "down into the recre-ating silences," for me a literal experience because my "where" of prayer in the morning is the basement. I descend to the silence of the basement so that my life can descend into the depth of my own heart and join Christ there in the place where my life is "hidden with Christ in God" (Col. 3:3).

But the process doesn't start in the morning. It begins at 10:00 PM when I stroll past my wife reading in the family room and tell her I'm going into the kitchen to get the coffee ready to brew at 5:50 the next morning. That's her warning that I'm about to go to bed. Then I go to the bedroom, take off my watch, which has two alarms set for 6:00 and 6:15, and put it on the bookcase about five paces from my side of the bed.

Six o'clock AM—the first alarm goes off. I walk over, grab the watch, and bring the watch back to bed with me. It goes off again at 6:15. Sometime between 6:15 and 6:30 I get out of bed, grab my Bible, journal, and a sweater, and head to the kitchen, praying I remembered to hit the auto-brew button on the coffeepot. The aroma that greets me tells me that I did. "O Lord, open my nostrils, and I shall praise you for coffee." I fix my coffee, then descend into the cold basement.

I turn on the heater (remember, polar vortex), sit down in the green La-Z-Boy, and put a quilt over my legs. I read the psalms for that day, then I flip to the Gospels. For fifteen minutes or so I do the kind of *lectio divina* discussed in chapter 1, dwelling with scripture, reading it, chewing on it. Letting it chew on me.

Keep in mind this important point: The way the practice of silence has been packaged and the way you can learn similar practices in non-Christian contexts often rips silence out of its natural home in the context of other forms of Christian prayer—especially praying the Psalms and *lectio divina*. Silence doesn't stand on its own, but it lives in life-giving mutual relationship with the other practices that make up a prayerful life of attentive availability to God.

A timer on my watch is set for thirty minutes. When I finish praying the Gospels, I start the timer, toss the watch in my lap, pull the quilt up to my neck, fold my hands in my lap beneath the quilt, take a deep breath in and out through my nose a couple of times, and then start. In my mind I say "Je-" on the in-breath, and "-sus" on the out-breath. "Je-sus." Slowly. "Je-sus." Three or four times, five if I'm lucky, before my mind starts thinking about the papers I have to grade that day or the van I have to take into the shop or the chapter on silence I'm supposed to be writing but which I can't quite get organized. A parade of thoughts—a boring thought, an angry thought, an anxious thought. My stomach growls.

Then I recognize that I'm thinking. Do I say, "Rats! See, you are a failure. You can't even repeat your word for one minute without getting distracted. You should have given this up a long time ago, buddy!"? No. As soon as I recognize what I'm doing, I release the thoughts by gently returning to my word: *Jesus.*

Eventually, while still saying my word, I hear footsteps. Ginger going to get coffee. Simeon, our ten-year-old, dashing into the kitchen after her. Mary Clare padding along the hallway. Silas—I don't hear him; he's practically a ninja. But I'm not thinking about these things. These noises—like the whir of the electric heater and the clicking of the furnace—are just so much flotsam and jetsam floating down the river, and I let them go by. I'm saying my word.

TRY THIS
Find a place. Set an alarm for ten minutes, and practice silence. Journal about what this time was like.

Then this thought: *My watch must be broken. I've been here for an hour! Will it ever beep!*

Recognize. Release. Return.

Finally, muffled by the quilt, a faint, "beep, beep, beep" sounds. I turn the timer off, say a few prayers slowly, and start to stretch. My mind gets busy again, but this time I don't need to release these thoughts. Fortunately, I don't need to cling to them either or fear them or perhaps most importantly, mistake them for the real me. They no longer become the lens through which I view the world, the center from which I live. I'm learning to stay in touch with a deeper center: Christ living in me.

I have this sense as I climb the stairs and emerge into this life of mine, this "active life," that the silence accompanies me. The silence is becoming my companion because the silence itself is the very God who rests in the depths of our souls and in whom we rest. Of course, this Silence comes with me.

## KEY TAKEAWAYS

Though we feel drawn to a silence so rare in our culture, the outer distractions and the inner chaos of our lives make us flee silence. And yet, practicing silence is like climbing into the lap of God, resting against God's breast, becoming one with God's heartbeat. So it's worth trying. We enter silence in many ways. This chapter introduced one way—the four *Rs*—repeat, recognize, release, return. As you begin to practice silence, remember these aspects:

- *Don't worry about doing it right.* There are several approaches; the key is to try one and stick with it. Be gentle on yourself when the going gets tough.
- *Don't judge your thoughts.* When we judge our thoughts or get angry and frustrated by distractions, that's just more thinking pulling us out of the silence. Instead, simply let go of the thoughts by returning attention to the prayer word.
- *Don't neglect a "where" and "when."* If you are going to practice silent resting in God, you need to have a clearly designated time and place. Establishing these is a key step to beginning and continuing the practice.

# 4

## THIS MORTAL FLESH
### *Embodying Our Spirituality*

When I started practicing body prayer I had to get up early—couldn't risk the neighbors seeing me.

When I stand in the den of my house and look out the wall of windows, I can see into my neighbor's dining room. I can wave at them while they eat their Wheaties. What would they think if they saw me in my den doing what could only look like bad liturgical dance? Especially since I was their pastor.

I wasn't ready for them to see this; it was too new for me. It's one thing to get a glimpse of your pastor reciting the Psalms or meditating on scripture or even sitting in silence. It's another thing entirely to witness your pastor, still in his flannel pajama bottoms, white T-shirt, and old green cardigan, twisting, spinning, and raising his arms. If they saw me, my credibility would plummet.

But I had to do it. Just a few weeks after sensing the word of *Let Me be your Teacher*, I presented lectures at a retreat in Arkansas. Another presenter lectured on spiritual practices. One practice mentioned was that of body prayer. I could talk a good game about theology and the body. One of my lectures addressed the restoration of our bodies to their rightful place in the practice of faith. But I had resisted putting my own theology into practice. After her talk, the time had come.

Like most of us, I have lived Christian history's ambivalence about our bodies; I have felt alien to my own body. But I began to see in that group of people at the retreat—old and young together, standing and moving freely, offering their bodies to God as a "living sacrifice" as Paul tells us to do (Rom. 12:1)—that our bodies are a gift through which we can learn from Jesus. They are one of the "givens." With our bodies we pass the peace; we sing; we eat the bread and drink from the cup. Our bodies let us rest on the sabbath and offer a cup of cold water in Christ's name. We live our faith through our bodies.

We can run from our bodies (metaphorically) and try to practice a faith tilted toward mind, soul, and spirit alone. Or we can accept the gift—along with the fear it brings for so many of us for whom our bodies cause deep anxiety or whose bodies have been the site of trauma or whose bodies are simply growing old and weak. An older woman warned me, after I had given a rather optimistic lecture on the body: "Some of us look in the mirror in the mornings and say, 'That's not me.'"

The woman assumed that since I was younger, I didn't understand this. But with arthritis pain and morning stiffness in my hips, spine, and shoulders for almost two decades, I wanted to tell her I understood. On many mornings, after hobbling over to the mirror, I could have said as well, "That's not me."

But it is me, and there's no escaping that. The body is part of being human. And through our bodies Jesus can be present to us, speak to us, form and teach us. Jean Vanier, the founder of the L'Arche communities, said after weeks of recuperation following a physical breakdown due to exhaustion, "I wasn't listening sufficiently to Jesus in my body, and so at one moment my body said, 'Stop.'"[1] How many of us are listening?

I came home from that retreat with a renewed commitment to offer myself by offering my body to God, to pray and praise with flesh and bone, to move without fear, to pray with my body.

And not to let anyone see me—least of all, church members.

## CHRISTIAN AMBIVALENCE ABOUT THE BODY

Christianity has had, at best, an ambivalent relationship with the body throughout its history. Though belief in the Incarnation—God's becoming an embodied human being—stands at the heart of our faith, some of the most vigorous debates in the early church revolved around how to understand Jesus' body and the role our own bodies played in our faith and salvation. One of the early beliefs, later rejected as inadequate, came to be called Docetism, which comes from the Greek word that means, "to seem." Advocates of this belief said that Jesus only *seemed* to be human—he wore humanity as a kind of disguise.

But why would these advocates promote this view? Because as Christianity moved from its Jewish roots into Greco-Roman society, it moved into a more dualistic culture that tended to value soul over body, a culture influenced by the philosophy of Plato and his interpreters. Many early Christians felt deeply sympathetic to this cultural perspective and believed it unseemly for any divine being to become tainted by contact with creaturely flesh. Thus, Jesus only *seemed* to be human.

The opening lines of the Apostles' Creed state that we believe Jesus was "born of the Virgin Mary." Contemporary debates focus on whether or not Christians believe in the virgin birth. We find it hard to imagine that some in the early church took issue not with the word *virgin* but with the word *born*. Being born is messy. To some early thinkers it didn't seem right that a divine being should become sullied by undergoing human birth. The early Christian writer Marcion argued that Jesus, though human, descended bodily from heaven. He wasn't *born*.

My favorite example of early Christian skittishness about the body comes from a second-century Gnostic writer named Valentinus. He said, "Jesus endured all things and was continent. He ate and drank in a manner peculiar to himself, and the food did not pass out of his body."[2] What kind of divine savior would have to take a potty break? There was a deep-seated aversion to imagining Jesus undergoing these kinds of bodily processes: birth, urination, defecation.

As a Gnostic, Valentinus fell in a broad category of people who saw the human problem as one of embodiment: We are really souls that need to be freed from our bodies so we can return to the purely spiritual realm from which we came. (If that simply sounds "Christian" to you, it shows how this Gnostic way of thinking still influences us.) Some Gnostics even believed that the world was created not by God—why would a purely spiritual God create matter?—but by a kind of demigod or demon who enslaves spiritual creatures in created bodies. We needed a spiritual savior to rescue us, but a body couldn't imprison him too or how could he save us? For the Gnostics—then and now—spiritual disciplines and practices provide ways of taming the body in order to free the soul.

What became orthodox Christianity prevailed. We profess in our creeds that we believe in "One God" who "created" all that is, "seen and unseen." In other words, matter—creation—was made by God and is good. We also say we believe that Jesus was born, suffered, and died and that he was raised bodily from the grave. We say we believe in the "resurrection of the body"—that is, not only was Jesus raised bodily, but we too will be raised bodily. Paul says we'll be raised with "spiritual bodies"—and it's hard to know what that means. The Bible and Christian theology teach that human beings are not just souls waiting to get out of our bodies and back to God or to heaven, but that we are only completely human as body-soul unities. A soul without a body is not a human. A body without a soul is a corpse. We are bodies, and God meant us to be that way.

But we still live with this legacy of ambivalence. When I served as a pastor, I got more questions about the resurrection of the body than any other part of Christian belief. "I thought we were immortal souls that went to heaven when the body died," people would say. While it's hard to say what a resurrected body will be, Christianity is clear on this point: Salvation is not just for souls. We are being saved and will be saved body and soul.

Our bodies matter in our faith. Our bodies matter in our spirituality. Our bodies matter in our prayer. Our bodies matter in our learning to follow the way of Jesus, in our receiving and responding to his transforming love for us.

But the resistance runs deep.

## DEEP RESISTANCE

I know the resistance runs deep in me. I discovered it palpably and by surprise on a retreat with some clergy colleagues.

Eight other pastors and I had been meeting several times over a two-year period to learn how to be more faithful spiritual guides in our congregations. Two trusted guides led us—one, a retired Baptist pastor, Larry, who late in his career began practicing spiritual direction and found that this gave him a new perspective on pastoral ministry, and the other a nun, Sister Joanna, who served as a Catholic campus minister at a nearby university.

At one of our retreats the schedule indicated an evening exercise called "anointing prayer" led by Sister Joanna. When I saw it, I didn't think twice. I'd been in many healing services where we anointed people on the forehead with oil before praying for them. But looking back, I should have known it wouldn't be so simple. After all, Sister Joanna often stretched us beyond our comfortable patterns of prayer.

I should have anticipated that it would be more interesting and dangerous than the anointing prayer I'd been used to.

Arriving first to the meeting room after dinner, I noticed strange things in the room, items we didn't use in our church when we anointed the sick. On a corner table stood a stack of clean white pillows, and, next to them, a stack of fluffy white towels. My subconscious began sending fear signals through my body before my conscious mind even knew what was going on. And then I saw the offending item: a large bottle of oil—*not* anointing oil. The sticker on the bottle was all too clear: this was *massage* oil. Pillows, towels, and massage oil—this would not go well.

My fight-or-flight reflex kicked in, and since there was no one there to fight, I began to consider flight. My eyes darted around the room looking for a way out. My heart pounded so hard you could see the rhythms of its palpitations shaking my shirt. My hands began to sweat. My mind began to whirl. There was only one thing I could think, and it wasn't *What are we going to do?* It was *How am I going to get out of this?*

But the other participants began to file in. They looked too serene under the circumstances. (Only later did I learn of their fearfulness; they have good poker faces.) We sat in our circle, and Sister Joanna began to explain the activity. We would pair up (yikes!), sit facing each other knee to knee with the pillow on our laps (this was going from bad to worse), and then we would massage each other's hands while Sister Joanna led us in a guided meditation.

When Sister Joanna told us we would pair up, I scanned the room. I didn't want to engage in this activity with a man, however strong our friendship was, and the women—well, that seemed almost inappropriate. I feared how this would end as Sister Joanna began passing out postcards, cut in half and shuffled. We would find the person who had the other half of the postcard we held and then sit down knee to knee.

That's when I got my only reprieve—I was paired with Sister Joanna. My one lucky break.

It would take a lot of money and several hours with a therapist to understand all my reactions that night. But at the heart of it lay an anxiety about bodies—my body and other bodies, and especially the intimacy that comes with touching (nay, massaging) each other's bodies. And I am convinced that some of it came from the way many Christians, including me, have been schooled to fear our bodies. To imagine that we could bring our bodies into Christian community with touch becoming a prayerful expression of our relationships with one another and with God—this possibility didn't register.

That retreat exercise set me on a journey. How will this journey begin for you? Will it begin in fearful anxiety? Will it seem utterly natural? How would you have reacted in such a context?

Thinking about our bodies is complicated and confusing. Our relationships with our bodies, our fears and inhibitions and anxieties, are complex and deep-seated. It's possible we grew up in homes where our bodies—their integrity, privacy, and care—were not respected. So we have no sense of when and how we can offer our bodies to God as a holy offering.

> CONSIDER THIS
> How would you have reacted when told about the hand massage exercise? Why?

It's also possible that our bodies have been violated and abused. While Jesus spent a great deal of his ministry healing bodies, he also ministered to people whose bodies had been violated or whose physical conditions caused them to be shunned. And, in the end, he himself was the victim of physical violation, abuse, and, finally, murder. I believe that God is a tender God—acquainted with pain and understanding of our fears. If bringing the body into your practice of faith is a subject of deep anxiety for you, find a person you trust with whom you feel secure and safe and ask for help. The journey to

TRY THIS
Write a few paragraphs about your body. How have you treated it? How has it been treated by others? How does it feel to think about your body as part of your relationship with God? Pay attention to the emotions that arise as you do this exercise.

receiving the gift of your body will take time and requires the support of trusted companions along the way.

My journey has taken time. As I have reflected on my anxiety and fear that night with the massage oil, I have come to see my anxiety as an invitation to make this a place of discovery, to be intentional about this part of my journey with Christ. We experience Jesus' presence in our fears and desires to flee as well as in our joys and moments of peace. As I look back, I hear in my anxiety an invitation to open—slowly and safely—this gift of my body and to discover how my body, mind, and soul can be a place of communion—communion with others and with God. My body can be a way of prayer. Through it, Jesus can speak to me, and I can respond.

## BEGINNING THE JOURNEY—AWARENESS

A safe way to begin involves awareness. Don't start thinking, *I have to do something new.* Don't buy a book on body prayer or sign up for a workshop on the body. Begin simply by awakening to all the ways your body already is one way you receive and respond to the life of Jesus. Notice how your body already composes a part of your spiritual formation.

Take worship. If you've visited many churches for worship, you have probably noticed that worship often seems aimed at our minds: a focus on understanding concepts, on hearing words, especially in mainline Protestant churches. But even words are physical, and hearing is embodied. When the apostle Paul said that "faith comes from what is heard" (Rom. 10:17), he was talking about our bodies.

So even if you worship in a place where you mostly sit and listen, you can still pay attention to your body. Do you ever stand, kneel, cross yourself, or bow? Do you shake hands with a person in the pew during the passing of the peace, dare to offer a hug, or to "greet one another with a holy kiss" (2 Cor. 13:12)? How about singing, an enormously physical endeavor? One reason I have always loved to sing and to sing heartily in church is that singing offers the most natural way for my body to participate in praising God.

And then consider the sacraments. A *sine qua non* of a sacrament entails something physical—bread, wine, water. We break bread with our hands, hold it with our fingers, let it dissolve in our mouths. We feel the rush of saliva in our mouths as we taste the wine. All of this happens despite our particular sacramental theology. Churches have different ways of making sense of what occurs in a sacrament, but most believe that sacraments are physical signs and actions through which God makes divine grace present to us. Christianity may have a two-thousand-year-conflicted history with the body, but as long as worshipful acts we call sacraments have existed, the body has never been far from our faith practice.

You can begin to find it at the heart of your faith practice by paying attention to how your body is already involved in your worship.

Once we gain more awareness of our bodily participation in worship, we can notice our bodies in other places as well. When I'm washing dishes, I sometimes pay attention to my hands in the water, allowing the sensation to remind me of my baptism and the cleansing, healing nature of God's grace. When my body feels tired and sore, I can let

DISCUSS THIS
In your worship communities how are your bodies part of worship? Can you think of ways to increase bodily participation?

its pain and fatigue remind me of my dependence on God; let it teach me that God did not make us to be machines for accomplishment but wants us to experience renewal through rest and play. I can notice that wrestling with my boys or scratching my daughter's back or rubbing my wife's shoulders allows me to share blessing with them. Once we wake up and pay attention to our bodies, we realize the many surprising ways they are already part of our lives with God.

Finally, if we engage in any kind of service, it involves our bodies. At the Last Supper, Jesus gave a precedent for Sister Joanna's anointing prayer when he performed the intimate act of washing his disciples' feet—Jesus on bent knee, the disciples exposed and vulnerable. Some denominations take Jesus' command to wash one another's feet literally, but most see in his action a symbol of lives of self-offering that Jesus expects of us all the time. When we volunteer at a soup kitchen, offer a cup of cold water to one of the "least of these"; when we visit prisons or shut-ins or the sick—we offer our bodies to them and to God at the same time.

As I write this it is spring. In the past few days devastating tornadoes have crossed the Midwest and Southeast, destroying hundreds of homes. I know people in North Carolina in the churches where I've pastored who are already organizing work teams. Many of these people wouldn't be caught dead in a prayer group or in a spiritual formation group; but when it's time to push a shovel or swing a hammer, they are ready. They may not think of it this way, but it's true nonetheless—when they shovel debris and swing a hammer, they are worshiping, offering their bodies as living sacrifices to God and to others. They are responding to Jesus with their flesh. They are practicing the prayer of the body.

## BEYOND THE BEGINNINGS—INTENTIONALITY

We can take another step beyond awareness to intentionality. Once we gain awareness of our bodies—how we are (and are not) offering our whole selves to God in worship, discovering our fears and inhibitions—we can proactively welcome our bodies into the life of prayer.

I took this step at the retreat in Arkansas that I mentioned at the beginning of this chapter. I saw clearly that the time had come for me to unwrap the gift of this "given" and stop being afraid. Even though I lectured at the retreat, I allowed myself to become a participant as well. I was in a safe space, and I couldn't have asked for a better guide. Jane, the other presenter, is a remarkable retreat leader.[3] Her steady, soothing voice speaks with great gentleness and authority. She has been teaching prayer so long and inviting timid people to explore aspects of their lives they've been afraid of forever that she knows all the pitfalls and fears, the obstacles and the excuses. And so she expertly invited the retreatants to be intentional about their bodies in prayer, and I willingly followed.

Jane introduced us to what she calls a prayer of intention.[4] We know that our minds wander. They forget things; they struggle to focus. But she told us that our bodies have their own kind of memory. We might, for example, think about our intention to live peaceably with our neighbors but minutes later find ourselves screaming at a slow driver on the freeway. We lost our intention. But we can also enact our intention with our bodies—allow them to represent a sacrament of intention. We can move our bodies in gestures that symbolize the life of prayerful love we believe we are being called to. That movement of our bodies can become a part of our prayer practice just like chanting the Psalms, reading the Gospels, and sitting in silence.

After her presentation I rushed back to my room, opened my journal, and began to write about the shape of life and prayer I had sensed God calling me to. I knew receptivity was part of it. Thomas Merton rightly states, "It is God's love that warms me in the sun and God's love that sends the cold rain. It is God's love that feeds me in the bread I eat and God that feeds me also by hunger and fasting."[5] Or, as others have put it, every moment is a sacrament of God's love. I wanted to be increasingly open to receiving that sacrament.

God was also calling me to share my life more fully with others—not just through preaching and writing but by being less fearful of connection and intimacy and allowing myself to be known. I also wanted to be a grateful soul, to follow the example of saints who displayed gratitude throughout their lives. If each moment is a sacrament of God's goodness, then I wanted not only to receive that sacrament but to give thanks for it.

Finally, I wanted joy. God calls each of us to joy. "Rejoice in the Lord always" (Phil 4:4), Paul says. I keep nearby when I pray a picture of Saint Francis who took Paul's injunction quite literally. His feet are off the ground, his arms are extended to the sky as he jumps in freedom and joy. The picture portrays a man who worships with his body, who loves the creation, and who is not afraid to let the joy of the body show.

Receptivity, self-offering, gratitude, and joy—the four prayers I would embody.

TRY THIS

Find a place where you can be alone, and begin to experiment with gestures that express the shape of life and prayer you long for. Why did you choose the gestures you chose? What do they mean to you?

I stood in my room and began to experiment with gesture and movement. *What felt comfortable? What seemed natural? What gestures and movements could express my prayer, desire, and intention to live these four prayers?* The process of developing body-prayer movements was like trying on shoes—some looked nice but didn't fit. Some gestures seemed like they would be perfect but felt awkward. I had to find the movements that were right for me—no one else could do this work. Fortunately, it didn't take long. I wove the four gestures into a kind of dance and then repeated them over and over, sometimes changing the order. They became the chords on which I improvised a song of prayer with my body. Though it felt strange, I knew this could become part of my prayer.

## WELCOMING THE BODY TO PRAYER

The flannel pajamas are the same. And I've still got the same white, now rather holey T-shirts. When it's chilly, I pull out the same green cardigan sweater that used to be my father's, the one that matches the La-Z-Boy that, as you know by now, is such an integral part of my life of prayer.

But this year my family lives in a different house with different neighbors who live down the hill from us so they wouldn't be able to see me anyway, even if they were looking. But I wouldn't mind now if they did; and if they asked me what I was doing, I could say without a hint of embarrassment, "I'm praying."

When the silence ends, I toss my quilt to the floor and stand. Before heading upstairs I put my arms out with my palms up and bring them slowly together and up toward my heart in a gesture of receiving. Doing this, I sometimes picture the people in my life, my wife and children, especially. This one gesture says the prayer: *God, I want to receive the gift of them. Life with five people in a small house tends toward annoyance and frustration. But I want to receive them in each moment as gift. If the annoyance and frustration are there, as they are bound to be sometimes, let me receive that too as a mysterious sacrament of your love. All things, each moment. May there be no more good fences that keep me from receiving.*

And then I put my arms out and swing them around, twisting at my waist like the sower throwing seeds indiscriminately. The seeds are my own life made available to those around me—those closest to me, of course, and students and colleagues as well. But also to those who interrupt my routines: to strangers, to those on the margins. I want to offer myself to the woman who sat outside the bookstore yesterday who wished my daughter and me a nice weekend, saying how beautiful she looked and wondering if I had any spare change. I don't usually have cash, but I have myself. *Lord, I have this bodily presence—how can I offer her that?*

My palms come together, and I raise my hands toward my heart in a gesture of gratitude for all I have received and will receive, for all I have offered of myself and the more of myself I will discover to offer. As my hands keep going up past my face toward the ceiling, they burst apart like fireworks—out, open, over my head in Saint Francis-like joy.[6]

A joy I don't need to wait for. It is here, incipient in this body now, in the freedom to offer myself, body and soul, to the One who made me and who offered his own body as a perfect act of love.

## KEY TAKEAWAYS

Christianity has a long, conflicted history with the body. We confess that Jesus is God in the flesh and that he died and was raised bodily from the grave. We also confess that we believe in the resurrection of the body. Officially, Christianity teaches that our bodies are crucial to our lives with God and salvation. But in practice, we have often shunned the body, believing faith only concerns itself with the soul. Recovering and practicing faith through our bodies can be anxiety-producing and fear-inducing, but it's worth it as we learn to offer our whole selves to God and our neighbors in love. As you begin to deepen your practice of spirituality through your body, remember the following:

- *Start where you are.* Begin by noticing the ways your body is already part of your spiritual life. Think especially about your body's involvement in worship. And then ask, How can it be more involved?
- *Pay attention to your body throughout your day.* Stop ignoring your body; let it speak to you. Notice when it's fatigued, for

instance, and consider what God is trying to tell you through that tiredness. How do you experience fear, joy, and love through your body?

- *Fear not—nobody is watching!* You can take steps to practice body prayer, shaping a prayer that is right for you without worrying about how it looks. Don't be afraid of looking silly—God is the only one watching, and God delights in these new steps you are taking in faith.

- *Talk to someone.* If thinking about your body causes serious anxiety and fear or if you have experienced abuse or trauma to your body, don't be afraid to talk to someone with whom you feel perfectly safe—a wise friend, a pastor, a counselor. There are people who can help you heal and become more at home with your body again.

# 5

## EAT THIS BREAD

### *Meeting Jesus in the Holy Meal*

My wife and I decided to be good denominational loyalists. We were visiting my brother, who lives in a large Midwestern city, and it was Sunday morning. Any other Sunday morning my wife and I would have been leading worship, but this was one of those rare Sundays when someone was filling in for us, and we got to choose where to worship. We chose, without much thought, to go to the downtown United Methodist church. Like I said, we're denominational loyalists.

The problem with having a Sunday to visit another church is that my expectations are way too high. With so few Sundays off, I always desire an extraordinary worship experience. (I'm such a consumer!) But we could tell, soon after arriving, that this was an old, declining church, propped up by an endowment. The facility was immaculate; a recent renovation made it completely handicap accessible. From the outside, with its imposing Ionic columns and its dome, it looked more like a county courthouse than a church. Only the cross on the top of the dome gave it away. On the inside, the sanctuary looked like a senate chamber with a wraparound balcony and several more columns that matched the ones outside.

If the building itself made me think my high expectations would be met, when worship started my hopes were deflated. Like a movie critic, I began to make my list: announcements—too long and folksy. The hymns—too slow. (I think my wife and I were the only ones singing.) The sermon, a week after the Boston Marathon bombings— blandly reassuring and vaguely comforting. I thought to myself: *If the mainline church is dying, this is "exhibit A" for why.*

I hate this critical part of myself. Worship is not a show to be reviewed. But it's hard to turn off my inner critic. In the same moment I was kicking myself with one foot for being so critical and with the other for coming here in the first place.

Then God kicked me, it seemed, and said, "Worship is not about you, Roger. It's about me."

That divine kick hit me when we got to the part of the service when the pastor stopped saying the things he'd made up that week and started saying the things the church had given him to say and doing the things the church had given him to do because Jesus said and did these things first. In other words, the time had come for Holy Communion.

Since the altar table was against the back wall, an usher pushed a makeshift altar table on wheels, prepared with the Communion elements, to the front of the sanctuary. The pastor took his place behind the makeshift table and spoke the ancient words I had said many times myself standing behind an altar: "The Lord be with you." And I responded instinctively, the response cutting short my laughter about the altar on wheels: "And also with you."

The Lord was with us and would soon give himself to us in a tangible way.

Tears unbidden streamed down my cheeks as we progressed through the liturgy. Hearing and saying familiar words and phrases make them easy to ignore. But that Sunday they served as a stark reminder to me: We didn't make up this story being told through these words and with these gestures and in the bread and the wine. It is God's story, the human story, and the story of how God chose in Jesus to make the human story *God's* own, so that God's story could become *our* own.

The story climaxes in Jesus' giving himself for us, in his dying and being raised again. Whereas the human story is a story of turning away from God, the story of this human Jesus is a story of relentless turning toward God, even if such turning to God gets him rejected and killed. He is at once God's turning to humanity and humanity's turning to God and God's continuing to give God's self to us in this act of worship, through these signs and ritual actions.

Jesus' words express it all: "This is my body, which is given for you" (Luke 22:19).

Why the tears? Because I clearly understood that I could list all the things wrong with the service (or arrogantly list all the things I would have done right); yet all the things wrong (long announcements, shallow sermon, slow hymns) could not prevent God's showing up, God's offering of self to us in Jesus, God's presence in this place—nor could all the right things guarantee it. Getting things right does not get God here. God is here because in Jesus, God has promised to be God for us. God's being for us in Jesus and with us in Jesus happens because God has promised, "This is my body, which is given for you."

What else could I do but stumble out of my pew, drunk with joy and gratitude and surprise, shuffle up the center aisle toward the altar on wheels, and extend my hands to receive this gift of Life, cupping them like a poor beggar seeking alms?

> **DISCUSS THIS**
> Tell your group about a time when sharing in Holy Communion touched you in a special way? Why do you think it did?

I might have been there because I'm a denominational loyalist. But God was there because God is loyal to God's own promises: *Not because of your best efforts nor despite your weak attempts at playing church will I offer myself to you. I do because I long to turn toward you and have you turn toward me. I show up because I have promised.*

How could I have forgotten?

CONSIDER THIS

When has your pickiness or preferences about worship distracted you from the real point of worship? What do you think the real point is?

Even if you are the one behind the altar, wearing the robes and waving your arms, the one who says the prayers and lifts and breaks the bread, it's amazing how easily you can forget the powerful simplicity of what's going on here: God is keeping God's promise to show up, offering God's self to us in Jesus, to give us life by pulling us into the story of God's life. Preoccupation with saying the words right, with lifting the loaf high enough, or adjusting your stole can distract from the simple heart of this sacrament.

And now that I'm more often sitting in the pew than standing in the front on Sundays, I see how we all forget, lose focus, get distracted. So much to think about and look at that the very act of worship meant to open us to God can appear a mere ritual.

## SEEING GOD'S BODY PRAYER

We are in good company, I realize, as I sit in a hard wooden pew in a great, towering church in Durham, North Carolina. It is the third Sunday of Easter, and the Gospel lesson comes from Luke. At this church, when it's time to read the Gospel, an entourage of white-robed people with candles and crosses and one carrying a big Bible walk down the steps and into the center of the church to read the

Gospel lesson—a physical symbol of what I tried to say in chapter 1: These four books of all the books of the Bible stand at the center of our life.

The previous week we were in John's Gospel, in the locked room with the frightened disciples when Jesus appears and says, "Peace" and with Thomas when he demands to see and touch the wounds of Jesus (John 20:19-29). But this week we walk with two disciples on the day of the Resurrection. Evening approaches. These two are walking a number of miles from Jerusalem to Emmaus. When you are on a long walk with a friend, you talk, especially if you've heard rumors that another friend of yours who'd been killed isn't dead anymore.

And, as the story in Luke 24 tells us, Jesus himself appears alongside them and walks with them. "But their eyes," the scripture says, "were kept from recognizing him" (v. 16).

There they are, just like us—Jesus comes near to them, and they don't recognize him. Like I said, we are in good company. We could offer a million answers to the question, What kept them from recognizing him? Because I recognize myself in these confused and puzzled disciples, I would venture the guess that the excitement and fear occasioned by the puzzling story they hear about Jesus' being alive preoccupies them. We all know how preoccupation can keep us from seeing clearly what's right in front of our faces.

I'm preoccupied here this morning as I listen to this Gospel story being read in church. My family has returned on a brief trip to the city where we lived for many years. We have already met lots of folks who have told us stories about life in town since we moved away, and I am thinking about them. My three tired kids are wiggling in the pew next to me, and I'm trying to keep them moderately still and quiet without being a total grouch about it. I'm glancing around the sanctuary to see if there's anyone here I recognize. I'm preoccupied like the clueless disciples out for a walk.

But then in the Gospel story, the two disciples arrive at their destination and invite the stranger who's been walking with them to stay because it's almost evening. And in this famous and familiar scene, Jesus the guest becomes the host. He takes the bread, he blesses it, breaks it, and gives it to them, and then, as the Bible says, "their eyes were opened" (v. 31).

The two didn't recognize Jesus by his voice on the road. They didn't recognize his clothes or his eyes or his gait. But they recognize these four gestures: Take, bless, break, give. I'm guessing they'd seen them before. How many times had they gathered with him around the table?

And when these two go back to Jerusalem to tell the eleven disciples, the eleven must recall the last time they saw him do it, the time when these gestures took on special significance in the upper room. Jesus performed them at the Last Supper before he said, "This is my body, which is given for you." He showed them that he takes, blesses, breaks, and gives not only bread but his very self. He is the bread. This movement must have seemed like a dance to them, unmistakable. Take bread, bless, break, give. His whole life and meaning—summed up in four movements.

It occurs to me as I sit here and listen to this story being read that these gestures are like God's own body prayer. And in them Jesus acts out what it means to live a life offered to God—a life of prayer. But at the same time, this life is offered to us as well so that we might receive the life of God.

In John's Gospel, the disciples recognize Jesus when he shows them his wounds. In Luke they recognize him when he shares the bread with them because in those acts he shares himself.

And he still does.

Because these gestures are so influential, when I teach people preparing to be pastors how to celebrate Communion, I tell them to make the gestures big; don't be afraid to use your arms. So many students and pastors approach Communion timidly. Perhaps they fear that by making a big deal out of taking, blessing, breaking, and giving the bread, people will mistake them for Jesus. But I believe this is how people will recognize Jesus being given to us in the sacrament. This will help us all wake up, refocus, recover from our preoccupations, and see into the heart of this meal—see the One who brings us to God and God to us by allowing himself to be taken, blessed, broken, and given.

Just like the celebrant now does on this third Sunday of Easter. She says the prayers with her arms stretched straight out; then she takes bread, lifts it high in blessing, tears it down the middle, and holds it out as if to give it to us.

The celebrant in her white robe and glittery stole is a petite woman with long hair and bangs that fall into her face. She's almost lost behind the enormously wide altar. I see her; but when she takes, blesses, breaks, and gives, I recognize Someone else who is giving himself to me. And that's the way it's meant to be.

## THE FOUR MOVEMENTS OF COMMUNION

Most of us know at least this one thing about Holy Communion: Every denomination and every local congregation celebrates it differently. And however your worshiping community celebrates it, I guarantee someone thinks it should be done differently.

There are the dippers, the common cup drinkers (with the priest who wipes the cup after each sip and finishes what's left after everyone has communed), and the "shot glass" drinkers. There are the flat bread breakers, the gluten-free advocates, and the Hawaiian bread lovers (usually children). There are the teetotaling grape juice users, and there are the winebibbers. There are the come-to-the-altar folks and the serve-it-in-the-pew folks. And any imaginable combination of the above. No wonder we miss Jesus, so preoccupied are we with these details.

And yet, beneath these (what I take to be) more superficial, if not irrelevant, differences, there is deep historical continuity among the ways many denominations celebrate Holy Communion. There's a good chance that each of several elements is present in your church's celebration in some way or another. When we begin to see these and pay attention to them, we take the first step in rediscovering Holy Communion at the heart of Christian spirituality. When we rediscover the Table as a place where God, through the grace of Jesus Christ, turns to us and turns us to God, then we can enter into the sacrament not as an empty ritual to be endured but as a feast of love to be savored. I want to draw your attention to four movements of Communion.

*First*: the story. Many churches call this the Great Thanksgiving, and, in fact, the word *Eucharist*—the word many churches use to name the sacrament—means "thanksgiving." In this sacrament we offer our thanksgiving to God. And the prayer usually prayed by the pastor or priest expresses our thanksgiving (so maybe we should whisper along with her). It also reminds us of what we have to be thankful for by rehearsing the story of God's "mighty acts of salvation," as some liturgies put it. If you pay attention to this prayer, you get the whole story—from God's creating us in God's image, to our refusing to live fully into that image by turning away in sin, to God's calling the nation of Israel to be a peculiar people devoted to God, to God's finally coming to us in the body of Israel's Messiah and God's own Son, Jesus.

The prayer usually recounts, at this point, the life and ministry of Jesus. Here's how one United Methodist Communion liturgy states it:

Holy are you, and blessed is your Son Jesus Christ. Your Spirit anointed him to preach good news to the poor, to proclaim release to the captives and recovering of sight to the blind, to set at liberty those who are oppressed, and to announce that the time had come when you would save your people. He healed the sick, fed the hungry, and ate with sinners. By the baptism of his suffering, death, and resurrection you gave birth to your Church, delivered us from slavery to sin and death, and made with us a new covenant by water and the Spirit.[1]

92

What a jam-packed prayer! And to think, through this sacrament, when we eat and drink in faith, we get to be on the receiving end of this world-changing, life-transforming ministry of Jesus. Holy Communion reminds us of the entire story of God's salvation, and we taste it for ourselves.

*Second*: the words of institution. It's hard to imagine a celebration of Holy Communion without a recitation of the words and the reenactment of Jesus' gestures at the Last Supper. They appear in three of the four Gospels and in First Corinthians and are standard in every Communion service. The whole service leads up to this, the focal point: Jesus' own words, telling us that in the breaking of the bread and in the drinking of the cup, we his followers receive him. We can let the theologians argue about how this happens—how Jesus is present: in what way, exactly, "this" is "my body." Isn't it enough for us to know that in the bread and the wine, somehow, Jesus is offering himself, his life, and his forgiveness—indeed, an entirely new relationship with God—to us?

A *third* element invokes the Holy Spirit. The one saying the prayer invites the Spirit to be poured out on the gathered people and on the gifts of bread and wine. As we say in my church, "Make them [the bread and juice] be for us the body and blood of Christ, that we may be for the world the body of Christ, redeemed by his blood."[2] We pray boldly for a dual transformation: Transform the bread and wine into Christ's body (let's not worry about how), and transform us—the very people in the room—into Christ's body so we may continue to share him with others and one another throughout our lives. When we consider what we are actually asking of God in these prayers, I begin to wonder, *How can we be so preoccupied through this?* We should be amazed and a little frightened.

A *fourth* movement involves the elements of Holy Communion themselves. Jesus came to us in a human body, flesh and blood. It won't do then to have a merely "spiritual" way of encountering him. As I said in the previous chapter, Christians have never been Gnostics, at least not officially. And most of us are not Quakers who have managed to avoid controversy about the sacraments by not having any. No, Communion encompasses real life, real-world stuff. So we use the real life, real-world food of bread and wine. These real-world elements of life become the conveyers to humans of the equally real-world life that God wants to give us, longs for us to receive, and wants us to become for others.

TRY THIS
The next time you are in a service of Holy Communion, pay attention to these four aspects. Do you recognize them? How obvious are they? Discuss with your group your observations.

This is what I mean when I say *what we need is here*. On Sundays and weekdays, all over the world and probably not more than a few blocks from where you are now, people gather around a table and give thanks for the story of all God has done. They recognize the saving life, death, and resurrection of Jesus in words and gestures, invite the Holy Spirit to transform them, and receive in a tangible way the life and presence of God through ordinary food and drink.

A pilgrimage to holy shrines around the world would be nice, sure; but a pilgrimage to a table in a sanctuary down the block is enough. More than enough.

## DEEPENING OUR EXPERIENCE

I was giving the welcome in worship one day, and I said something to this effect, "I hope you experience God in our worship today." Later that afternoon I received an e-mail from a thoughtful seminarian who had visited church that morning. She raised questions about my use of the word *experience*. "I'm wondering what you mean by 'experience God.' I don't think so much about experiencing God in worship because I believe in the objective presence of God to us in the sacraments. It's about God's really being there, not my subjective experience." Honestly, I hadn't given my words that much thought.

Reflecting later, I appreciated the woman's point. So often we are preoccupied in worship. We're in a rush to get to church; we've argued with our kids on the way out the door; we're not sure what's for lunch later; and we carry the routine stresses of life with us all the time. How wonderful to think that God's being present for us when we gather does not depend on whether or not we are preoccupied. After all, Jesus walked with the two disciples on the way to Emmaus even when they didn't recognize him. Only later do they realize that their hearts were burning even then, though their minds were someplace else.

As a minister and as a Christian, I *do* want to experience God. I want my whole self to know I've been in God's presence—mind, heart, and body. And never more than when I come to the Table. I taste the bread and the wine. I hear the words of thanksgiving. I pray along, asking the Spirit to transform me. And I desire transformation—my real life changed by a real-life God. I want to experience.

And I suspect you do too. We often become restless searchers because what used to help us sense God's presence doesn't help anymore. So we dash off, looking for something new. But another option exists. We can try to rediscover the practices we are used to, practices like Holy Communion. One step, as I suggested in the previous section, involves knowing more deeply what's going on; looking for the deep infrastructure of the ritual, an infrastructure that's largely the same across different traditions. Now I want to offer four words that can guide you into a deeper experience of this gift of communion with God: *attention*, *intention*, *longing*, and *often*.

*Attention.* When I attended that downtown Midwestern church, I focused my attention on everything that I thought was wrong. But at the right moment God's grace awakened my attention to what was true: God's promised presence in the sacrament. We can train our attention; we can learn to control it. And here is the simple invitation:

During the celebration of Holy Communion, as often as you need to, draw your attention back to what's going on. Keeping your eyes open might help. Watch. Look at the loaf, study the cup. Watch the pastor's hands. Listen to the voice. Pay attention to the prayers. Are they the same as the last time? Do they fit with the liturgical season? Do they reflect the scripture passages for the day? Noticing these things—paying attention in these ways—can draw us in more deeply to what's going on.

*Intention.* Intention accompanies attention. Through our heightened attention we can notice what's going on out there; being intentional means paying attention to what's going on inside of us. Why are you here? What are you thinking about? Is your intention to receive God's forgiveness at the table? Are you here because you think God will like you more for showing up at church and at Communion? What is your intention?

As we begin to notice our intentions, we can start to shape them. We can walk intentionally, knowing that as our feet move up the aisle toward the altar, we are being drawn close to God. As we cup our hands to receive the bread, we can let that be an act of intention, symbolizing our desire to receive whatever God has for us in this sacred meal. When we kneel at the rail and pray following Communion or when we cross ourselves, we can take these actions with our full presence and with deep intentionality. By awakening our attention and by shaping our intention we can improve the chances that we will make the same startling recognition the disciples made at Emmaus: It's the Lord!

*Longing.* If you've begun reading the Psalms, you have no doubt noticed a theme: longing. And that theme finds its fulfillment at this Table. In the Psalms, images of food and drink often illustrate the theme of longing. Read Psalm 63; 104; or 107. Our souls long for God as a deer longs for flowing streams. But when we fill our minds and hearts with other emotions and things—fear, anger, images from television and popular media—sometimes we don't notice our own longings and our emptiness. And if we don't notice our longings and emptiness, how can they be met at this table when God—as food—feeds us and fills us? I always invite parishioners to come forward with their hands cupped and extended as physical symbols of their longing for God, their hands forming an empty reservoir of flesh waiting to be filled by the bread of heaven. If you have been a restless searcher yourself, you are acquainted with longing. Recognizing that longing and bringing it with you to this meal moves you a step in the direction of satisfaction.

*Often.* This aspect may be the most controversial of all. Some of us grew up in churches that celebrated Holy Communion four or fewer times a year. When the upstart pastors came and tried to change it to monthly Communion, we revolted: "If we do it that often it won't be special." When I hear that comment, I often reply, "The next time your spouse wants a kiss, tell him or her

> CONSIDER THIS
> How aware are you of your attention, intentions, and longing as you partake of Holy Communion? What could you do to develop each?

you will only kiss four times a year, so it will be special that way." And then I mention what I once heard: Psychologists now correlate the daily "ritual" kisses in the morning and the evening with long, happy marriages.

Coming to Communion doesn't always have to be a mountaintop experience. It can serve as a regular, sustaining part of a relationship with God. It doesn't have to be boring and rote. When we bring our heightened attention, our honed intention, and an awareness of our longing for God, each time we come to the Table can be special. But it doesn't have to be. It can also signal God's and our enduring faithfulness to each other.

We can take comfort in God's promise to be for us and give God's self to us in Jesus even when we remain preoccupied. We can also be thankful that many ways exist to approach this sacrament that help us enter more deeply the mystery of God's love given to us.

## LEAVING THE TABLE

And one more thing—that prayer after Communion:

> Eternal God, we give you thanks for this holy mystery in which you have given yourself to us. Grant that we may go into the world in the strength of your Spirit, to give ourselves for others, in the name of Jesus Christ our Lord. Amen.[3]

Just as I have to get out of my recliner in the morning, go up the stairs, and get on with the day, so too in worship we have to leave. We get up from the Table and, as Christ's body, the church, we offer ourselves to others. The weekend I visited my brother and worshiped at a downtown church, I was annoyed by and critical of worship. But at the Table ,God fed me despite myself. I got to meet and receive Jesus.

And I also got to respond. I couldn't stay all day. I had people to love. It was time to go.

## KEY TAKEAWAYS

In Holy Communion, a universal Christian practice, God offers God's self to us, making divine love, grace, and forgiveness available through Jesus. So often, though, we are distracted or confused about what this sacrament means. By recognizing the four movements of Holy Communion and learning to increase our attention, hone our intention, and notice our longing for God, we can deepen our experience of the sacrament. Remember this:

- *Rest in God's promise.* God's presence in worship and in Holy Communion doesn't depend on our getting everything right.

God promises to be with us, offering self to us in Jesus, even when the hymns are too slow and the prayers are mumbled. Take comfort in the promise of God's presence and grace.

- *Keep your eyes open.* If you watch as well as listen during the celebration of Holy Communion, you will have a fuller experience. Our minds may be preoccupied as we listen to familiar prayers with our eyes closed, but watching can help us notice and better understand what's going on.
- *Notice your longing.* The next time your worshiping community celebrates Communion, pay attention to your longing for God. How can you receive the bread and the cup that symbolize your longing for God's presence, grace, and forgiveness?

# 6

# THE WOUNDED BODY OF CHRIST

## Finding Jesus at Church

It may be a blasphemous thing to suggest, but sometimes it seems God made a mistake. God made the church the body of Christ, a sign of God's redemption in the world. God gambled on the church. Did God lose the wager?

You don't have to spend much time perusing the religious headlines to think the answer is yes. I live in Pittsburgh, a city that has been an epicenter for mainline Christian dissension over homosexuality. When the Presbyterian Church (USA) decided to let individual presbyteries (regional bodies with dozens of churches) choose whether they would allow the ordination of homosexuals, several Pittsburgh churches left the presbytery. In 2013 forty-six Presbyterian churches either left the denomination or closed their doors. Since 1980 the PC (USA) in the several counties around Pittsburgh has lost 55 percent of its membership.[1]

Conflict and decline isn't the worst of it. When we consider the pedophilia scandal in the Catholic church, scandals regarding megachurch pastors, and the ongoing reality of racial segregation in many denominations, we wouldn't be too far wrong to ask incredulously, "Is this the group of people God has said will be a sign of the presence of God's reign on earth and bearers of the good news of God's salvation?" Talk about a scandal.

The perspective doesn't change much at the local level. Two weeks ago I was the guest preacher at a church that only two years ago installed large screens on which the words of the liturgy and hymns could be projected. During the prelude, the lay worship leader who sat next to me facing the congregation, leaned over and said, "It's different, having the screens behind me. I guess I'll have to look at the bulletin and the hymnal. The good news is, after the early service, someone told me the images on the screen were too dark. At least that means they were looking at the screens."

"Was their installation controversial?" I asked, failing to practice worshipful attention during the prelude.

"Several people swore they wouldn't come back if we had them installed."

When local churches are held hostage by threats and gridlock over technology, we often wonder, *What was God thinking?*

We can point to churches that feed the poor, build Habitat houses, engage in acts of racial reconciliation and community building. I pastored a church that housed homeless men and women for one week every three months, fed them, played with their kids. The United Methodist Church has been waging a campaign to stamp out malaria in Africa and has made great progress. Good experiences abound.

CONSIDER THIS

Does negative news about the church cause you to doubt whether God is at work in the church?

What happens when we put the scandals, divisions, dissensions on one side of the scale and the good works on the other? I don't know which side would weigh more, but it still leaves the question: Couldn't God have done a little better?

Maybe at Pentecost instead of sending the Holy Spirit—granted, a necessary burst of energy and mission there at the beginning—the Holy One should have sent an organizational consultant—someone to help us get our act together.

As bad as it seems sometimes, we can't escape the theological reality: The church is the body God has called the body of Christ. This human organization embodies what Paul calls the "mystery of Christ" in the letter to the Ephesians (3:4). Among and through the Christians you see every day and on Sundays, the people you eat with at potlucks and serve with on committees, the people you avoid and the ones whose hands you eagerly shake, Christ can make himself known, present, available. And you can respond.

Believe it or not.

## PEOPLE—THE BURDEN AND THE BLESSING

It happened often. People would visit the church my wife and I pastored. They would be taken by the warm hospitality, inspired by the sermon, moved by the worship, and decide *This will be my spiritual home.* And everything would go swimmingly for a year. They would get involved in service projects, make friends, and finally (or fatefully) they would get nominated to serve on a committee. They would accept with enthusiasm, with some pride at having so quickly moved into the ranks of those governing the church (oh, how eager are the new!). After about six months, we wouldn't see them again. They had encountered the church's blessing and bane: people. And they left.

Living in Christian community as the church comes easy when it involves showing up once a week, getting spiritually fed, and volunteering for service projects that make us feel good about ourselves. But as soon as we move "inside" where people make decisions about budgets, strategic direction, and facility use, among other things, the glamour disappears. The spiritual glow we saw from afar fades, and we discover the aura of drudgery clinging to the church's life. And the faint of heart slink off to a different church (or no church) where they can have that good feeling again, untarnished by the reality of dealing with people.

Here's what I think folks mean when they say they are "spiritual but not religious": They want to benefit from religion (the benefits of which are amply attested to in the psychological and medical literature) without having to deal with the messiness of real people. We have to deal with people in our families and at our work—why mess up religion with them? We don't want institutional religion, and what is an institution but people living together, working together, and making decisions together in order to sustain common commitments and a common project?

In the interest of full disclosure, I will say that as a pastor, I too have pined off and on for a church without the people!

But when God gave us the church, God gave us one another. And in learning to get along, getting aggravated, reconciling, negotiating competing agendas until we can learn to let go of our agendas, the constant rubbing of one ego against another until we realize our egos don't matter so much as we thought, we find what we need: a community where Christ uses other people in our lives to make us more like him.

Ruth Burrows writes, "There is an asceticism involved in silence and solitude, as in community living"[2]—what I call asceticism of community. In the convent, Burrows says, asceticism has a communal aspect. *Asceticism* is the word that refers to the disciplines and practices that aid us in being more receptive to the work of God's transforming love in our lives. Usually we think of individual practices—fasting, prayer early in the morning when we'd rather be sleeping, anything that has an element of self-denial. Living in community can be a kind of asceticism. Burrows notes that many times we would rather not be with other people or with the particular people we are with. We find them boring or aggravating. (Are you thinking of specific people in your life yet?) We'd rather be alone. Or the people somewhere else seem more interesting, so we would rather be with them. However, in a convent inhabitants commit to the people with whom they share life over the long haul. God puts them with this particular community, even if they'd rather be someplace else. Burrows writes, "To expose ourselves generously to the demands of community life; to refuse to shirk them in any way is to expose ourselves to God, allowing Him to purify us through others, shatter our illusions with humbling self-knowledge, divest us of everything selfish and enable us to love others with a pure, mature disinterested love."[3]

In other words: Community exists for our salvation—the "purifying, sanctifying effects of community life."[4] If we refuse to run away, we will discover what we need. Community life wears away our self-wills so that our lives can be more in tune with Christ's will.

Benedict of Nursia, the father of monasticism in the Christian West, didn't write the first monastic Rule. However, his was certainly the most influential rule over the centuries and the one that has most shaped monastic life to this day. At the beginning of his Rule, Benedict mentions several different types of monks, one of which he calls "gyrovague" monks—monks who move from one monastery to the next, never settling down. Benedict declares that they are self-indulgent and gluttonous because they never have to have their wills bump up for long against the will of another.[5] Every time they move to another community, they think they will find the perfect one—the one where they will finally fit, be understood, and happy. And as soon as their illusion is shattered, they move on, never realizing the perfect place doesn't exist.

It's not just monks. I have met gyrovague pastors as well. Parishioners too.

Real growth in the spiritual life doesn't happen until our first inclination to flee these people and find better people becomes an invitation to stop and ask, "How is Jesus giving himself to me—transforming me—here, through my relationship with these people, and how can I respond?" And as we choose to stay, resisting the urge to become gyrovagues, we can take some comfort in the sure fact that God is using our annoying peculiarities, flaws, and even sinfulness to help others grow as well.

That's life as church.

**CONSIDER THIS**
Reflect on your own life in the church. How have you experienced both the burden and blessings of the people in a local congregation?

Dietrich Bonhoeffer, the German theologian, articulates both the blessing and the challenges of living in community. Bonhoeffer believes that among the services we owe brothers and sisters in community is the service of bearing one another's burdens.[6] "Bear one another's burdens," Paul writes, "and in this way you will fulfill the law of Christ" (Gal. 6:2).

Bonhoeffer states that before we can bear one another's burdens, we must learn to "bear the burden of one another."[7] We must bear one another as burdens! In their freedom, other people will always be a burden to us. Bear. Don't flee or judge. Bear—a bedrock rule of community life. Bonhoeffer writes, "God did not make others as I would have made them. God did not give them to me so that I could dominate and control them, but so that I might find the Creator by means of them."[8] God gives us God's very self—Jesus offers himself to us—through the burden of being with others in community.

After worship ended one Sunday, I took my place in the narthex to shake hands and listen to people say, "Nice sermon," and "Enjoyed your talk." I recognized a woman standing to the side, waiting to talk to me, though I couldn't recall her name. She belonged to the church where my wife had been an associate pastor several years earlier. She walked toward me. "Hey, good to see you again," I said, stretching out my hand.

"I enjoyed worship today," she said.

"Well, it's good to have you with us."

Then she told me why she was here. "The personnel committee at the church where I'm a member made some decisions I don't like, and some of the people have really bothered me. So I might be worshiping here for a while."

I wanted to be welcoming and hospitable, so I said, "Certainly, you are always welcome here."

Here's what I felt like saying, but didn't: "The chances are good our personnel committee will make decisions you object to, and someone here will begin to bother you—maybe me! So you might as well stay where you are. Jesus is meeting you there through those people, I have no doubt. If you run away, you might miss him."

Maybe she figured it out for herself; she never came back.

## THE GIFT OF FORGIVENESS

Lest this sounds too negative, there's another way we receive and respond to the gift of Jesus through one another in the church. By offering forgiveness we can be Christ for one another.

In his memoir *Telling Secrets* Frederick Buechner describes the oldest part of the Tower of London known as the White Tower, which was built by William the Conqueror in the eleventh century. The second floor of the tower has a small chapel called the Chapel of Saint John. Bare, simple, silent, still. "You cannot enter it," Buechner says, "without being struck by the feeling of purity and peace it gives."

But just beneath the chapel lies the most terrible of all the tower's dungeons. It measures four feet square by four feet tall, so a prisoner can't stand up in it. A heavy oak door blocks out all light and air. Almost no air to breathe, almost no room to move. The dungeon is known as the Little Ease. Imagine finding yourself in the Little Ease.

And then Buechner writes, "I am the White Tower of course."[9] And so are we. But instead of living in the peaceful chapel, we live in the dungeon, locked in and afraid. Afraid our secrets will be found out. Afraid we will have to account for the wrongs we have done.

Afraid, most of all, that God will finally track us down and wag a divine finger in our faces and say, "After all I have done for you, how could you?" Anything—even living in an airless cell—would be better than that.

Every year when Easter comes around, we in the church read John 20, the story of the disciples who are afraid and locked in a room after the Resurrection. I think of the Little Ease. The Bible says they are locked in "for fear of the Jews." I think they also fear that the one they abandoned and watched being led to his death will burst through the door, now risen, and say, "How could you?" They fear being found out.

DISCUSS THIS
Share with one another a time when you experienced living in the Little Ease. What, if anything, helped you out?

This image of the disciples locked in the house, afraid, depicts all of us—all humanity—because we are all there with them, betrayers and deniers, people who have heard so many times throughout our lives, "How could you?" We feel sure God will ask us that question next. When the Christian tradition states that all people are sinners, it doesn't mean that we do a bad thing every once in a while. It means we are trapped, unable to live in the hope and abundance God wants for us because we have done wrong, and we fear being found out.

But that's not what Jesus says—even if the disciples deserve it. That's not what he says when he tracks them down and mysteriously appears in the room with them.

Jesus shows them his wounds. The disciples' abandonment of him had real consequences. They played a part in his death. Their sin and ours nailed him to the cross. These wounds—caused by humankind's rebellion.

But "How could you do this? How could you let this happen to me?" did not accompany Jesus' showing the wounds. Instead he offers a word of forgiveness and reconciliation: "Peace be with you" (John 20:19). That word acts like a key. It reaches into the disciples' hearts and unlocks their prison doors of fear and guilt. They know their guilt, and they know they are forgiven.

And then the disciples rejoice. Their posture of fear turns into a posture of praise. Then they can be glad they saw the Lord. Then they can say as we sing on Easter Sunday, "Hallelujah!"

I think Charles Wesley captures the moment in a verse of one of my favorite hymns "And Can It Be That I Should Gain": "Long my imprisoned spirit lay, fast bound in sin and nature's night; thine eye diffused a quickening ray; I woke, the dungeon flamed with light; my chains fell off, my heart was free, I rose, went forth, and followed thee."[10] The disciples, cowering in a dungeon of their own making, hear Jesus' word of peace as an invitation to leave the dungeon and enter the peace of the chapel above.

But here's the best part: After the disciples rejoice, liberated as they are from fear and guilt by Jesus' greeting of peace, their lives change forever because he gives them a new vocation. He doesn't simply invite them to walk out; he *sends* them out. He breathes on them the Spirit. The same Spirit that anointed him at his baptism when he began his mission now anoints them as they begin their mission to take Jesus' word of forgiveness into the world, offering it to neighbors, strangers, and one another. "As the Father has sent me, so I send you" (John 20:21). Their commission: to forgive sins.

> TRY THIS
> Make a list of people for whom a word of forgiveness from you would be liberating. What next step do you have to take to offer that word?

As church community, we too have been commissioned to announce the words of Christ's forgiveness to one another. This is how Christ has chosen to offer himself to us. Now it's our job, yours and mine, to walk into the dungeons of fear and guilt as Jesus did. It's our job to walk into the rooms where people cower in the corners, afraid of hearing "How could you?" Now it's our job to speak words of peace and reconciliation, to announce God's forgiveness. That's the gift we can give one another.

Lesslie Newbigin, a missionary and theologian of the last century, commenting on this passage and on the new commission the disciples receive (John 20:21-23), wrote that Jesus is giving "a commission to do something that will otherwise remain undone: to bring the forgiveness of God to actual men and women in their concrete situations in the only way that it can be done so long as we are in the flesh—by the word and act and gesture of another human being."[11]

By a word, an act, and a gesture of forgiveness, we can be Jesus for one another.

My brother Bo was leaving the hardware store with his twenty-month-old son Graham. He had to change Graham's diaper before they drove away. While changing Graham's diaper on the backseat of the car, Bo let Graham play with the car keys. His only mistake: forgetting to get the keys back. After he buckled Graham into his car seat and loaded his purchases into the trunk, Bo reached for the front door handle of the car. Graham, playing with the keys, hit the door lock button. Instantly every door locked. Bo was on the outside; Graham was on the inside. And Bo began to panic.

Bo called his wife who worked ten minutes away. "Get down here; Graham is locked in the car." Then as they waited, Bo screamed to Graham through the window, "Push the other button, push the other button." He figured he had about a 50 percent chance that Graham wouldn't push any more buttons, a 25 percent chance he would hit the panic button, and a 25 percent chance he would hit the unlock button.

Bo banked on the possibility of Graham freeing himself. Before Bo's wife arrived, Graham pushed the unlock button and was free.

Someone working at the store saw the whole thing and asked, "Kid get locked in the car?"

"Yeah. But he got himself out."

"Well, if it ever happens again, there's a locksmith just a block up the road. He gets kids out for free."

In the church, we are not only burdens for one another; we serve as God's locksmiths for one another. Unlike Graham, when we lock ourselves in the house of fear and guilt, when we are suffocating in the Little Ease with no light and no air to breathe, we can't get ourselves out. We have no magic button to push. But a locksmith can show up who remembers how it feels; a locksmith can show up who has been set free; a locksmith can show up who's been baptized and anointed and commissioned by Jesus himself. A locksmith can show up—a pastor, a small group member, a neighbor in the pew who passes us the "peace of Christ"—and with a word or an act or a gesture can make real God's forgiveness, can unlock the doors, can lead us out.

> CONSIDER THIS
>
> When has someone acted as God's locksmith for you by unlocking your dungeon of fear and guilt?

Bonhoeffer says that when Jesus gave the disciples the commission to forgive sins, "Christ made us into the community of faith, and in that community Christ made the other Christian to be grace for us."[12]

It happens on Sunday morning when the community gathers for worship. I saw it often when my wife, Ginger, led worship—the most significant, amazing thing we as a congregation did. Ginger would stand and lead worship attenders in a prayer of confession. We say in general ways the things we've done that we shouldn't have done and the things we should have done but didn't do. Then in the silence that follows, we add our own personal touch. *I lied. I stole. I cheated.*

*I ignored someone. I broke confidence. I did what I've always done, and I hate myself for it.*

Then Ginger looks up and says what this commission in John 20 allows her to say, "In the name of Jesus Christ, you are forgiven." But it's not just Ginger making this pronouncement—if what Jesus says is true. It's Jesus himself using the voice of this pastor.

And then members of the congregation respond (because this commission is ours as well): "In the name of Jesus Christ, you are forgiven." But if what Jesus expresses is true, then it's not just us saying it but Jesus himself speaking through us.

That's life as church too. Unlocking the door of the Little Ease for one another.

## Soul Friend in the Pew

We meet and respond to Jesus when we rub against others in community. We receive the forgiveness of sins when brothers and sisters offer words and gestures of pardon in community. In church community we also encounter Jesus' abiding presence, the fulfillment of his promise to be with us always, as we discover soul friends. The most helpful thing I've done in my life of prayer is to spend one hour once a month with an older, wiser Christian who is experienced at prayer and living life with God.

In one way, prayer is natural—we were made for it and we long for it. In another way, we find prayer confusing and fraught with challenges. Why not spend time with someone who knows the way and who can give gentle guidance, encouragement, and support? In the church God has given us these people.

A soul friend walks alongside us, the way Jesus walked with the disciples on the way to Emmaus. A soul friend companions us. A companion is one who breaks bread with us—the way Jesus broke bread with the two disciples after they reached Emmaus. A soul friend is one who offers the word or gesture of forgiveness, one in whose presence we are not afraid to bare our souls.

Writer and educator Parker J. Palmer says that the soul resembles a wild animal. On the one hand wild animals are resilient, able to survive in adverse conditions for a long time. They are also shy. If you want to see a wild animal, he says, you don't go tearing through the forest shouting. Instead, you sit down, get still, and wait, and eventually the shy, wild animal, when it senses it's safe, will show itself.

The soul is like that, Palmer says.[13] If it is going to show itself, it needs a friend in whose presence it feels safe, a hospitable place where it can come out of hiding and let itself be known. A soul friend can create this kind of hospitable space for you.

One of the ways a soul friend displays hospitality comes in his or her ability to listen. I assigned a class to read my book about my former spiritual director named Larry.[14] I asked them to list qualities or characteristics they saw in my description of him. One of the first qualities listed was this: Listening. Deep listening. Larry has no agenda for the hour other than being open to hear what the Spirit is up to in my life, and that involves paying close attention to me: What I'm saying, how I'm saying it, what I'm not saying—a discerning listening. I may be telling a story, trying to get to the heart of a matter when I don't know what the heart is, and Larry will say, after his characteristic pause, "You know, I heard you say. . . ." And that's it, the heart of the matter. I said it, but I didn't hear myself say it until he heard it and said it back to me. That kind of listening combines gift and skill, and I know I am in the presence of mystery when I meet with someone who can listen that way.

Larry also listens for what authors and editors call the "through line," the thread in a book or a story that runs through the whole thing, that holds it together, and gives it direction. Even when a part doesn't seem to belong, somehow it's connected to the through line. And a soul friend listens not just in this one hour but week after week for the through line, believing that life is a story being written with God. So what is the story saying? What's holding it together?

Soul friends come in many varieties—sometimes a formal relationship called spiritual direction, sometimes informal. Reading this description may help you realize that you have a soul friend and didn't know it. Sometimes it's mutual. You serve as soul friends to each other, helping each other find the plot of the story God is writing in your lives. In any of these cases, together you practice one of the gifts of being church, knowing that "where two or three are gathered," Jesus is there too (Matt. 18:20).

If you want to open this gift of being church, consider making a list of people you know who could mentor you in a life of prayer. Ask your pastor if he or she knows of any spiritual directors. Keep your eyes open for friends or church members who may want to meet regularly and support one another in prayer.

## NO MISTAKE

It's Wednesday night. I'm at the dinner table with my family, but I'm not eating. In a few minutes I will leave for my small group that meets at the church. We always have a meal together, so on Wednesdays I don't eat at home.

We are a diverse group in age, race, and denominational background. But when we are together, we practice this gift called church. We learn to hear and receive and respond to Jesus through one another. We pray together. We sit in silence together. We share our burdens with one another. When the father of one of our group members died, we grieved with her and supported her. We may even be burdens to one another sometimes. And we offer Christ's reconciling peace to one another, more often through gesture and act than in word. We're still learning.

If we were trying to get our small church to grow by enticing more people to come, I doubt you would take our picture and put it on a billboard along the interstate. We wouldn't note the great meals, at least not when I'm cooking (we've had some good ones though). We wouldn't trumpet our wisdom or the depth of our discussions, even though it can get pretty deep. An outsider might fail to mention us altogether.

How strange, because this act of practicing church—along with the thousands of others around the world—is one of the best things Jesus has going on anywhere. No mistake about it.

## KEY TAKEAWAYS

Sometimes the news headlines about the church seem so bad it's hard to believe the church is really Christ's body. But the church can be Christ for the world even in its brokenness. We can be Christ for one another and the world by the way we bear with one another, being patient with people who annoy us and forgiving those who wrong us. The very gift of offering forgiveness lies at the heart of God's mission for the church. With a word, act, or gesture of forgiveness, we make tangible Christ's grace for another. We can also be Christ for one another by being soul friends. God has given other Christians the gifts of patience, listening, and acceptance. Having a wise soul friend can significantly influence our spiritual journey. As you think about "practicing church" as part of your spirituality, remember this:

- *Don't run away too soon.* People in the church will frustrate, annoy, and offend you. Rather than believing that this frustration signals a need to go elsewhere, try to envision your relationship with a frustrating person as one way God can shape you more fully in Christ's image.

- *Stay humble*. After all, you are probably the frustrating person someone else wants to escape!
- *Forgive*. Never underestimate the power of forgiveness. God has placed in your hand a rich, powerful gift that can transform lives and make God's forgiveness tangible. Don't be stingy with forgiveness.
- *Find a soul friend*. Seek out someone—a soul friend or spiritual director—who can accompany you as you practice Christian spirituality. Maybe God is calling you to be a soul friend for someone else.

# 7

## UNTO THE LEAST OF THESE
### *Being with the Poor*

Still a Midwesterner at heart, I have not acclimated to the Appalachian terrain of Pittsburgh. I feel rather insecure driving through the hills, never seeing the horizon, always wondering if there's a truck in my lane headed at me around the next corner. Add to that the fog, and it's a wonder I didn't stay home that night. One kid was sick, so the rest of the family was staying in. I'd had a long day at work and felt tired. Darkness had come and now fog. Between where I was and where I was going there were only hills. I had every reason to stay in but went anyway.

Driving through Fox Chapel I passed mansion after mansion. I couldn't see them that night but had seen plenty of them in the day. After several months of driving through this borough, my kids still point and gawk, acting like the Beverly Hillbillies when they see these houses. Fox Chapel is one of the wealthiest boroughs around Pittsburgh. Someone told me that it was zoned so that no lot could be less than an acre. No need for good fences to be good neighbors in this borough. The neighbors are far enough away.

My family and I don't live in Fox Chapel. We live in a nearby township with affordable homes, but we still enjoy the Fox Chapel amenities—library, parks, and schools. When we moved here we knew nothing about Pittsburgh, but many people touted the Fox Chapel schools.

I have to drive through Fox Chapel to get where I'm going. After a few miles, the environment changes. The way takes me down a long incline toward the Allegheny River. The houses get closer together until they stand only feet apart. Many of the houses are multifamily homes. Chain-link fences border the small parks. The streets grow narrow. Many storefront shops remain vacant, hopelessly wearing "for rent" signs.

I am entering the borough of Sharpsburg. I wonder if it's a place the new monasticism movement calls "abandoned places of Empire," places that seem overlooked, off the radar screens of urban renewal efforts.[1] It's one of the economically distressed areas around Pittsburgh. Close to Fox Chapel, the residents of Sharpsburg and Fox Chapel fall in the same school district, but our realtor subtly advised my wife and me to buy a house in the township on the other side of Fox Chapel so that our kids wouldn't attend the same elementary school as the Sharpsburg children. "A lot of parents prefer to live on the other side of Fox Chapel," our realtor said, "because a high percentage of children at this school are 'renters.' "

I arrive at my destination, a senior citizens center in Sharpsburg. Twice a month Faith United Methodist Church in Fox Chapel, where my family worships, hosts a meal in Sharpsburg. Inspired by the vision of our pastor, the members of the church started hosting a meal at the senior citizens center called "The Neighborhood Table." Our pastor, Tom, saw between Sharpsburg and Fox Chapel an invisible wall, the kind the gospel tells us has been broken down in Christ. More often than not, families that live in Sharpsburg and Fox Chapel will never become friends. They don't go to the same community events. They attend the same schools, but I've been told they don't associate when there unless they have to. And they rarely find themselves having a meal together. So the church, with no other agenda, started hosting a meal where those who came to eat could ignore the walls of class and race by living like they're broken down, which they are, and where unlikely friendships could unfold. A place and time where God could do something surprising and new. By the time I started going to The Neighborhood Table, they'd been having the meal for nearly a year.

CONSIDER THIS
How far would you have to go to eat a meal with people of a different class, race, or culture than you? What obstacles stand in your way?

One night our whole family sat and ate with all the children. I asked a kid named Nicholas where he went to school. "Dorseyville Middle School," he replied—one of the Fox Chapel schools.

"How do you like middle school?" I asked, trying to make conversation.

"I hate it."

"Why?" I asked.

"I don't like rich people."

The story of a relationship between two boroughs in five words.

Nicholas is the reason I got in the car that foggy night and drove to the senior citizens center, Nicholas and the others at The Neighborhood Table I've gotten to know. I want Jesus to be my teacher, and Jesus made it clear that he will be present to us through the people that those of us with money call "the poor"—even though they may not describe themselves that way.

But when we're having dinner together, I'm not sure who in the room are "the poor." I certainly feel poor knowing that an accident of birth, the stratified nature of our culture, and my own conscious choice to live where I live separates me from Nicholas and his friends. I also know that if I'm going to receive and respond to Jesus, then I need to be where he is, among the people in whom Jesus says he will meet me.

## THINKING DIFFERENTLY ABOUT SERVICE

I don't volunteer to serve the meals, clean the tables, or stand outside and welcome the guests at these meals. I don't sign up for any doing. I come to eat and talk, which is a change for me. How I got to this place where I'm no longer interested in what we in the church call "service opportunities" is part of my journey of rediscovering the heart of Christian spirituality.

I took great interest in these possibilities when I pastored in Durham, North Carolina. Being a church known for "serving the poor" has a certain appeal. I wanted people to get involved, to sign up to serve. I hated for a week to go by when we didn't provide an opportunity for people to serve. I wanted the church members to say, "Come this Saturday to the Habitat build. Sign up this week to serve a dinner when homeless families stay at our church. Stay after worship today to fill flood buckets to send to the hurricane-ravaged coast." My view of service, rooted in my sense that the church should love its neighbors, was tinged with utilitarianism: Providing easy opportunities for people to serve offered a great way to involve folks in the church.

Not to mention that my church had to report to the conference at the end of each year statistics that would suggest something about our church's vitality: "How many people have been involved in hands-on service projects this quarter?" I wanted the number to be as high as possible.

Moreover, the demographers keep telling us that younger generations want a life of significance. They want to make a difference. I wanted to give them a church where they could feel like they were making a difference. And the folks making a difference are the ones who serve. Who would ever think that my showing up at a free community meal in order to eat and chat is really making a difference?

Fortunately, I wasn't the only one casting vision for ministry in the Durham congregation. We had on staff a young Minister of Adult Discipleship and Witness named Reynolds. He had no interest in utilitarian programs; he had interest in finding Jesus by being with the poor. At one point, I began to worry that the church lacked focus and opportunity for service. I believed we needed an annual mission theme to focus our church's service and get the community's attention. I went to Reynolds and said, "Make this happen. We've got to get the community's attention; make a difference; we've got to do something."

Reynolds thought about that for a while and then said, "Maybe we should do it the way Jesus did, by spending time with our neighbors, by learning simply to be with them."

So we launched our first annual mission theme: "Who Is My Neighbor? Living, Learning, and Listening with Our City." That theme moved us away from the paternalistic assumption that we know the hopes and needs of our neighbors and that we show up and do *for* them—an assumption that has driven so much of the wider church's thinking about mission and service. Rather, we hosted dinners where we listened to the hopes and needs of our community. We sponsored a local Pilgrimage of Pain and Hope where we learned about the ongoing legacy of racism in Durham and our part in it. We had cookouts on the lawn to which we invited our neighbors so that we could begin living with them without an agenda. Our action moved beyond mere busyness to a response directed by God's choice to be with us in the incarnation of Jesus.

DISCUSS THIS
What does service look like in the church you attend? When has your service kept you at a distance from those you serve? When have real relationships emerged?

A story illustrates the old way of thinking about service. One Christmas the men's group from my church in Durham volunteered to give toys away at the rescue mission's annual Christmas toy distribution. At the event, the men (all white) from our church stood behind a plastic orange fence handing toys to parents (mostly African American and Hispanic) who couldn't afford to buy Christmas presents for their children. The parents didn't choose the toys; we distributed them according to each child's gender and age. Many of us left feeling uneasy. Our service seemed to replicate the divides of race and class that have plagued our city, and we remained strangers to those we helped.

Something felt wrong, symbolized by the orange fence. We served but with no possibility of relationship. We would not see the eyes and the smiles of excited children—or the frowns and tears of the disappointed ones getting a toy they never would have wanted. The dignity of Christ makes us truly human and ultimately valuable—and neither side of the fence would see that dignity in the other.

I now believe that the biggest difference we can make in the world is to be in places where unlikely relationships can form, where rich and poor together can learn to see in each other the guiding Spirit of Christ, and where our mutual service can flourish. This service grows not out of paternalistic assumptions and happens at a distance but out of knowledge of others' needs, hopes, and dreams. When we find ourselves offering service this way, we will be learning from Jesus, receiving and responding to him.

That's why I don't talk about service much anymore. Maybe that seems too extreme, since Jesus talked about service. But our service often prevents the possibility of relationship. Jesus' understanding of service grew out of the relationship he expected his disciples to have with one another and those they served. Until our service starts to look like his, I'm not sure of its usefulness. I'm increasingly drawn to more exciting, unusual, and risky possibilities for all involved—the kind of unlikely friendships that can form when churches decide to eat with their neighbors who are just a few miles away but worlds apart, the kind of relationship that can form when we gather around a table with no agenda.

And with no orange fences.

## "Being with" Our Neighbors

Samuel Wells and Marcia Owen have given me the language to make sense of this new perspective in their book *Living without Enemies: Being Present in the Midst of Violence.* It's simple language—the language of "being with."[2] They note different "models of engagement" that can shape how we think of service. The first they call "working for." The "working for" model involves an imbalance of power, skill, and initiative. One group of people—usually with greater wealth and access to resources—tells another group of people what their problem is and proceeds to solve it for them. Wells and Owen say this is the "conventional model of engagement across class and race boundaries."[3] This is the soup kitchen model, the Christmas toy giveaway model. This model maintains a clear "us" and "them."

Wells and Owen also mention a "working with" model. In the "working with" model, others are invited in to imagine the solutions to their own problems and to work for them. Habitat for Humanity, for example, employs an element of "working with." Those who get a new house contribute to building the house and have a mortgage to repay. It's not one-sided work. I believe this model of engagement still supports an imbalance of power and resources, still an "us" and "them," and the initiative usually focuses on the "us." And yet this model promotes the *possibility* of working together.

But Wells and Owen offer another model, more difficult than either of the above and harder to understand: "being with." As they put it, "Being with is not fundamentally about finding solutions, but about companionship amid struggle and distress. Sometimes the obsession with finding solutions can get in the way of forming profound relationships of mutual understanding, and sometimes those relationships are more significant than solutions."[4] The latter claim—that relationships are more significant than solutions—is hard for many in our American activist culture to swallow. How could relationships be more significant than solutions?

In Ephesians 2, Paul outlines what we might call the "trouble with the world." And the trouble with the world is that people are cut off from one another: there are Jews and Gentiles. The most meaningful aspect of Christ's work came in breaking down the dividing wall between these people and creating one new humanity. As Paul says, Jesus "is our peace" (Eph. 2:14; see also vv. 11-22).

We don't think of the world's problem as being the relationship between Jews and Gentiles. But the church believes its mission is to embody the new humanity. We affirm that endemic divisions in our society are directly at odds with God's vision of a restored creation. We experience too many dividing walls. "Working for" and "working with" can leave dividing walls in place, barriers that, if crossed at all, are only crossed for a time. But Paul refers to the "church," which embodies the mystery of a people who are reconciled to one another—who can feast together across lines of race, class, gender, and ideology. They learn to see and respond to Jesus' invitation: "Find me not in isolation but in this new relationship; this is where I am. And when you can see me in each other and in these new relationships, then a divided world can see me in you." That is significant.

Who knows? A solution to a problem may emerge along the way.

Sam Wells and Marcia Owen relate how an organization called the Religious Coalition for a Nonviolent Durham, of which Marcia is the director, learned to move from "working for" to "being with." The heart of the coalition's work involves hosting prayer vigils at the site of every homicide in Durham and organizing care teams called Reconciliation and Reentry Care Teams. These care teams partner a person coming out of prison for a violent offense with a team of five or six people from a local faith community to help the former inmate reenter society. I served on the first care team the coalition started.

Men and women coming out of prison face enormous hurdles. They struggle to find work; few employers want to hire convicted felons. They strain to pay rent, get their driver's licenses, reconnect with family—the list of obstacles is very long. They have to relearn how to function outside of prison walls. I remember meeting Michael, who had spent many years in prison though I never learned why. The members of his care team hoped to get him reestablished. In many ways, we found ourselves "working for" Michael. We thought our job was to help.

> TRY THIS
>
> Think of a service ministry in your church, and then write about how the ministry would have to change to move from "working for" to "being with." How could that ministry be done differently?

One woman in our group, Ann, began to feel like a mother to Michael. A retired teacher, she started tutoring him, teaching him to read. She relished the task of shopping for him, the challenge of finding clothes large enough to fit. She baked for him. She visited him. She loved him.

So when Michael stole a four-wheeler to buy drugs and got sent to a state prison so far away we could not visit him, it devastated Ann. The team met to talk about what we had been through with Michael, and Ann wept. "We failed," she cried. "We failed." Over and over again: "We failed." And at the time, I agreed.

But looking back, I wonder, *Did we?* If our job was to solve Michael's many problems—keep him off drugs, out of trouble, and in a good job—yes, we failed. But we didn't fail at our job of being with him—of learning from him, seeing Jesus in him, allowing our relationship with him to change us, becoming community with him. Maybe we didn't know him long enough to become true community.

But we found a space for the kind of relationship almost impossible in our society, one that crossed lines of race, class, and history. Michael was someone I had been trained to avoid, even to fear. And his culture and family probably trained him to fear people like me. Now the care team members live in the world as people who fear "Michaels" less and perhaps Michael lives with less fear of people like us. Now we live as people with eyes open to the possibility of being with one another when we hadn't been able to see that possibility before. I wouldn't call that a failure.

CONSIDER THIS
When have you failed at service? Does this story give you a new perspective on the meaning of success and failure?

Some organizations dedicated to serving the poor say, with a hint of superiority, "We don't give a handout; we give a hand up." This slogan states differently the meaning of the aphorism: Give a man a fish, feed him for a day; teach a man to fish, feed him for a lifetime. Giving a handout and a hand up have their place. Indeed, almsgiving has a cherished place in Christianity.

But neither is sufficient on its own, because neither makes room for the mystery of transformation the Spirit makes possible when we set aside our agenda and learn to be with one another. Whether I'm giving a handout or a hand up (as we thought we were giving Michael), I can't receive the sacrament of Christ's presence through the poor. And as long as I'm giving a handout and a hand up, how can they receive the sacrament of Christ's presence through me?

## WHO ARE THE "LEAST OF THESE"?

Matthew 25 contains the key text that allows me to say we can receive and respond to Jesus through being with the poor, that there is anything like a sacramental presence of Christ through the poor: "Inasmuch as ye have done it unto one of the least of these . . . , ye have done it unto me" (v. 40, KJV). This Bible passage seems to suggest that Jesus himself commands "working for" the poor—service as I've been suggesting we shouldn't understand it. What else could "doing it unto" mean but "working for"?

However, that way of reading the passage contradicts Jesus' own way of ministry. Jesus built relationships that transgressed cultural boundaries, eating with sinners and tax collectors. In other words, he partied with those our parents told us to stay away from. Indeed, he was one of the poor. "Foxes have holes, and birds of the air have nests; but the Son of Man has nowhere to lay his head" (Matt. 8:20). He did his "working for" the poor from the poor's side of the fence—as one of them.

Seminarians who have learned Greek enjoy preaching on John 1 on their first Christmas as pastors. That passage says the Word "became flesh and lived among us" (v. 14). They love to say, "In Greek the phrase 'lived among us' literally means 'pitched his tent.' In the Incarnation, Jesus 'pitched his tent among us' "—forgetting that the previous five pastors said the same thing. The meaning is clear: The Incarnation of the Word in the person Jesus Christ indicates God's refusal to work *for us*—to rescue humanity and transform creation—from a distance. God chose to be *with us* instead. Jesus' whole ministry follows this pattern: not saving from a distance but saving from up close.

Does Jesus' story of the sheep and the goats at the final judgment suggest a different approach? To those on his right hand, Jesus the king says,

> Come, you that are blessed by my Father, inherit the kingdom prepared for you from the foundation of the world; for I was hungry and you gave me food, I was thirsty and you gave me something to drink, I was a stranger and you welcomed me, I was naked and you gave me clothing, I was sick and you took care of me, I was in prison and you visited me (Matt. 25:34-36).

Now, the folks on the right hand are surprised. When, they ask, did we do these things to you? And Jesus answers, "Truly I tell you, just as you did it to one of the least of these who are members of my family, you did it to me" (vs. 40).

We can read that like a list of handouts—a straight-armed, from a distance, once a quarter show-up-at-the-soup-kitchen-and-stay-behind-the-serving-counter kind of service. Give food and drink. Give clothing. (Does donating to thrift stores count?) We can visit those in prison without building a relationship. Welcoming the stranger and taking care of the sick—that requires a little more "being with." But on the whole, this is "working for" service.

Until we discover the ambiguity of the phrase "the least of these who are members of my family." Who is Jesus talking about here?

The common interpretation states that Jesus is talking about members of the human family. Anytime we serve anyone who is sick, hungry, naked, imprisoned—the poor in the broadest sense—we serve Christ himself.

Another distinct possibility: The "least of these who are members of my family" refers to members of the Christian community. In that case, the world ("all the nations," v. 32) will be judged on whether they served Christ by welcoming the "members of his family," the church.[5]

DISCUSS THIS
Is this way of considering Matthew 25 new to you? Discuss what difference this alternate interpretation could make in the way you perceive of church and service.

We can read academic books if we want the scholarly arguments for the different positions. I simply suggest what could be a startling implication of the second possibility: The "least of these" are *already* members of the church. In other words, the service being talked about here is to the poor who are part of our community. What kind of church finds that the "least of these" are in its midst—not distant objects of charity but brothers and sisters in the pews? Undoubtedly a church that has learned to be with the poor in community and vital relationship, relationship that makes the kind of service mentioned in this passage possible to begin with.

Thomas G. Long, theologian and preacher, suggests the passage means both; we don't have to choose.[6] The beginning of a relationship may come in a visit to a prison or serving a meal. Maybe in this act the barrier begins to break down. But surely we learn to be in fellowship with one another, rich and poor together, serving Christ by serving one another. We feast not just at the sacrament of the Lord's Supper, but we receive the sacrament—receiving Christ—each time we open ourselves to one another in risky, vulnerable love.

## OVER THE HILLS AND THROUGH THE FOG

Here is why I would brave the hills and the fog: to receive this sacrament and in the hope that I myself will become a sacrament. That's why I eat with Nicholas and Samantha and Betty and Darlene and Joe. Are they poor? Am I poor? In different ways we all are. By grace we can be the "least of these" for each other as we eat our sliced ham, chomp our rolls, and wonder why the coffee is taking so long.

I serve if I'm asked. Sometimes not enough people have volunteered, and I need to serve a table. If the leader asks, I say, "Sure." That work must be done. Hospitality means that someone cooks, someone serves, someone cleans when the feasting is finished.

But as long as I'm choosing, for now I know where I need to be: where Jesus has the best chance of teaching me and where I have the best chance of learning. I take my place around the table, sharing the meal, learning to be community with new brothers and sisters whom race, class, and these horrible hills have too long kept from me.

## KEY TAKEAWAYS

Many of our ways of service—of working for or on behalf of others, especially the poor—keep us at a distance from those we serve and make it difficult for new, transforming friendships to occur. Jesus embodied a different way of service, choosing to be with the poor and the marginalized. If we are going to practice being with the poor at the heart of Christian spirituality, then we must find ways to do it that overcome the barriers of class, race, and geography, among many other barriers. When we do, we discover in the new gospel relationships that emerge that we can be Christ's presence for one another. Remember this:

- *Good fences do not make good neighbors.* To love the way God loved, we must step across the lines that divide, for through the cross Jesus broke down dividing walls to create a new humanity.
- *"Being with" is harder than "working for."* In our culture we are impatient to help and provide solutions. The way of Jesus, the way of "being with," involves having the patience to let unlikely friendships emerge that may provide solutions to problems as well.
- *We are all poor when we live in isolation from one another.* Receiving the presence of Christ in our neighbors—however much money they have or wherever they live—requires us to break out of our isolation, to brave the hills and the fog!

# In Closing

## Practicing the Heart
## of Christian Spirituality

Does your mother give you money on your birthday too?

This book began with a story about the way my restless search for something more—a deeper spiritual experience—often led me to binge-read spiritual books, hoping the story of another's life with God would inspire my own. I told how one Christmas, with one hundred dollars in my wallet—a birthday gift from my mother—I drove to a bookstore, eager to spend, until I heard a voice inviting me to put the brakes on my search. "Let Me be your Teacher," the voice said. I took that to be a message from God: *Roger, I am enough. What you need is here. Slow down the restless search, and return to me. Learn to receive and respond to my presence. I'm all you need.* And I had to take a concrete step to heed this wisdom: *Stop buying so many books on spirituality—at least for a while.*

Have you noticed the irony yet? You have come to the end of another book on spirituality! Since we don't know each other, there's no way for me to know how you came across this book. Perhaps this is the first book on the practices of prayer you've read in a long time.

Maybe you were responding to a voice that led you to this book, to read it to help you rejoin the journey with God with growing awareness and intentionality.

On the other hand, maybe you are a restless searcher like me. Maybe you bought this and a few other books with the money your mother gave you for your birthday, and as soon as you finish this one, you will move on to the next one and then the next and the next and the next.

Let me ask you, Having nearly finished, are you satisfied?

Of course, I hope the answer is yes. I hope this book has satisfied. I hope you enjoyed the stories, learned something about Christian spirituality, felt inspired to give some of these practices a try, grew in deeper relationships with the people you read the book with, even laughed a couple of times. I hope reading this book was satisfying.

But are you now satisfied ultimately?

The answer has to be no. *Reading about life* with God does not substitute for *living life with* God, with growing in your awareness and intentionality as you seek to receive and respond to Jesus who is both the journey's way and its end.

The seven "givens" at the heart of Christian spirituality remain. What you need really is here. Reading about them cannot replace practicing them. It can't substitute for taking those first few steps into the heart of Christian spirituality or deciding to deepen your practice as you continue to learn that God has given you everything you need and that God alone is enough.

So the rest of this book has one aim. To convince you it's time to put the book down, however glad I am that you read it, and to take some steps into the heart of Christian spirituality.

This book has been a signpost, pointing beyond itself to the way that God, through Jesus, offers God's self to us through these seven givens of Christian spirituality. The arrows have been hung on the post of my own story, but the details of my story are not what matter most. What matters is how you will begin living these practices, how you will end up with your own stories to tell of early morning prayer and driving to community dinners and bearing the burden of other church members.

What matters now? The concrete steps you will take to begin or deepen your practice.

At the end of this section, I offer two concrete suggestions for each of the seven givens. The first suggestion I call Beginning Step. Each Beginning Step exercise will provide a doable, bite-sized experience of that particular practice—a taste. Remember what I said earlier: Started is better than right. Doing something is better than not doing anything at all because you fear doing it wrong. These exercises will help you throw that fear to the curb and begin.

The second exercise I call Deepening Practice. You may have already tasted some of these practices if not all of them. These exercises aim to give you doable, concrete suggestions on how you can—as the name suggests—*deepen* your practice, expand your engagement with each of these practices, and weave them into your life.

In these practices God has given you what you need to receive and respond to Jesus' presence in your life. What we need is here. But how you wear these practices will look different. Only by trying, by taking these beginning steps and by deepening your practice, will you learn how you should wear them. They are like musical scales and chords; these are the basic scales and chords of Christian spirituality. But like jazz musicians, we won't all play them the same way. Rather, they are the scales and chords God has given you to improvise a life with God.

What will your song sound like?

## PURPOSEFUL RESTLESSNESS

I need to be completely honest: We will never be satisfied. The search never actually ends, even when we've found Jesus. The phrases *Jesus is enough* and *what we need is here* can mislead if they suggest a firm ending point—now we have arrived! We never arrive. Some early church theologians taught that the journey into God never ends, even in heaven, because God is infinite, and we are finite. We never finish exploring the depths of God's life and love. Gregory of Nyssa, a fourth-century theologian, wrote, "This truly is the vision of God: never to be satisfied in the desire to see him. But one must always, by looking at what he can see, rekindle his desire to see more."[1] Since God's goodness, God's triune life, is infinite, we will never be satisfied. We will always be restless.

But we can be restless in two ways: An aimless restlessness—the kind I talked about in the introduction, an aimless search for more for the sake of more wherever we can find it. My wife and I had a dog once with a highly undisciplined nose; she moved at the whim of her nose. She couldn't run across a field without sniffing aimlessly every square inch, zigzagging back and forth, making little if any progress across the field. She embodied aimless restlessness. We humans often set out in aimless pursuit of—we don't know what. Aimlessly restless.

But there is also a purposeful restlessness. Psalm 27 says, " 'Come,' my heart says, 'seek his face!' Your face, Lord, do I seek" (vs. 8). The search for God lies at the heart of what it means to be human—to search and long for. The gift God offers through these seven givens is that though our search will never end and our longing will never find complete satisfaction, our search doesn't have to be aimless. We can seek God's face; we can receive and respond to God in the face of Jesus even though our restlessness won't disappear. It will be a purposeful restlessness. It will have direction. There can be a steadiness to the search, a direction to the longing.

Practicing the heart of Christian spirituality through these seven givens offers that kind of direction. As they become woven into your life, indeed, as they become the frame that supports your life's growth in God, you will find your restlessness being increasingly aimed in one direction: at the face of God.

I remember one night helping my son Silas, who was seven at the time, spot the Big Dipper. Even though I pointed in its direction, his gaze went everywhere; he couldn't get his eyes on it. So I walked behind him, gently placed my hands on the sides of his head, and slowly aimed his face in the right direction. After he spotted it, we could have stood there all night marveling at the beauty and mystery of the stars. Who could tire of them?

When we give ourselves to these practices, these seven givens at the heart of Christian spirituality, we place ourselves in the hands of the Spirit. Through them the Spirit's gentle hands guide our gaze toward the face of God; they point our searching in the right direction.

And who can ever stop marveling, stop enjoying, stop gazing at the beauty, love, and life shining on us from the face of God?

## BEGINNING STEPS AND DEEPENING PRACTICE

### Meditating on the Gospels

*Beginning Step:* Establish a "where" and "when." Write them down—where will you be when you meditate on the Gospels, and when will you do it? Then take Mark 2:13-17, and spend fifteen minutes with it. Read it through once for understanding and then again, lingering over it as you meditate and then a third time, letting it lead you into prayer.

*Deepening Practice:* Do this every day at the same time and the same place for one month. Pick one Gospel and stick with it, and don't expect to read and meditate on more than two or three chapters in a week.

### Praying the Psalms

*Beginning Step:* Pick one psalm (try Psalm 25), and read it slowly to yourself out loud. Then give yourself fifteen minutes to rewrite the psalm, paraphrasing it in your own words, letting the psalm become your prayer.

*Deepening Practice:* Consider ways you can pray through all one hundred fifty psalms regularly. How can this practice fit into your life? Try this: For one month, before going to sleep, read slowly one psalm while sitting on the edge of your bed, beginning with Psalm 1 and ending with Psalm 30.

## Inhabiting Silence

*Beginning Step:* Establish a "where" and "when" (immediately after meditating on the Gospels is not a bad idea). Then spend five minutes a day for one week sitting in silence, practicing the four *R*s (see chapter 3).

*Deepening Practice:* Do this for four weeks, adding five minutes each week so that by week four you are sitting in silence for twenty minutes.

## Embodying Prayer

*Beginning Step:* The next time you are in worship, pay close attention to your body. Let yourself be deeply aware of your body's experience of worship. Pay attention to when and how you move; whether and when your body gets restless; what ways your body feels tired or invigorated in worship.

*Deepening Practice:* Write three words that succinctly express the shape of life and prayer you long for. Then spend some time alone experimenting with gestures (and don't feel limited to using your arms—use your whole body), trying to discover movement that seems to embody the words you chose. Reflect on this practice: How did it feel? Is this something you would try again?

## Feasting at Communion

*Beginning Step:* Review chapter 5 before attending a worship service with Holy Communion. Then pay attention during the Communion liturgy: Can you discern the four movements of Communion mentioned in chapter 5? Does the celebrant perform the four gestures—take, bless, break, and give? How are you invited to participate? Do you stay in your pew? Walk to the front? Kneel at the altar rail?

*Deepening Practice:* Ask a pastor for a copy of the complete Communion liturgy with all the prayers (it might be in your hymnal or your denomination's book of worship). Spend some time before a Communion service reading through the prayers, becoming more familiar with them. Ask God to use this practice to increase your attentiveness and availability during the Communion service.

## Practicing Church

*Beginning Step:* Make a list of five people in your congregation who frustrate or annoy you. Then pray that God opens your eyes to the ways that God can use your relationship with these people to help you see and respond to Jesus.

*Deepening Practice:* Find a soul friend or a spiritual director with whom you can meet at least monthly to discuss your life of prayer and your practice of faith. If you don't know where to begin, talk with your pastor or contact a professor of spirituality at a nearby Christian seminary for suggestions.

## Being with the Poor

*Beginning Step:* Have lunch at a nearby soup kitchen or homeless shelter. Stand in line and eat with the others being served. Learn someone's name and story over lunch.

*Deepening Practice:* Have lunch (or breakfast or dinner) at a nearby soup kitchen or homeless shelter once a week for a month. Try to eat with the same people as often as possible. Learn their stories. Share yours.

# NOTES

## Introduction

1. Augustine, *The Confessions of St. Augustine*, trans. Hal M. Helms (Brewster, MA: Paraclete Press, 1986), 7.

2. C. S. Lewis, *Letters to Malcolm: Chiefly on Prayer* (New York: Harcourt, Brace & World, 1964), 90.

3. Herbert McCabe, *The Teaching of the Catholic Church: A New Catechism of Christian Doctrine* (London: Darton, Longman and Todd, 2000), 72.

4. Athanasius, *On the Incarnation: The Treatise de Incarnatione Verbi Dei*, trans. and ed., a Religious of C.S.M.V. (Crestwood, NY: St. Vladimir's Seminary Press, 1996), 93.

5. Augustine, *On Christian Doctrine*, trans. D. W. Robertson Jr. (Upper Saddle River, NJ: Prentice Hall, 1958), 13.

6. James Whitcomb Riley, "The Hoosier in Exile" in *The Complete Poetical Works of James Whitcomb Riley* (Bloomington, IN: Indiana University Press, 1993), 670.

7. Wendell Berry, "The Wild Geese," in *New Collected Poems* (Berkeley, CA: Counterpoint, 2012), 180.

## 1   Red Letters and Wild Stories

1. Jerome F. D. Creach, *Violence in Scripture* (Louisville, KY: Westminster John Knox, 2013).

2. Ibid., 8–9. While reading the Old Testament symbolically is by no means the heart of Creach's approach, he does allow for this.

3. Walter Brueggemann, "Warrior God," in *The Christian Century* (Dec. 25, 2013): 30–31.

4. Thomas Aquinas, *The Aquinas Prayer Book: The Prayers and Hymns of St. Thomas Aquinas,* trans. and ed. Robert Anderson and Johann Moser (Manchester, NH: Sophia Institute Press, 2000), 5.

## 2   One Hundred Fifty Prayers

1. Martin Luther, "Preface to the Psalter," trans. Charles M. Jacobs, in *Luther's Works*, vol. 35: *Word and Sacrament*, ed. E. Theodore Bachman (Philadelphia: Muhlenberg Press, 1960), 254.

2. Dietrich Bonhoeffer, *Dietrich Bonhoeffer Works,* vol. 5, *Life Together* and *Prayerbook of the Bible*, ed. by Geffrey B. Kelly, trans. by Daniel W. Bloesch and James H. Burtness (Minneapolis: Fortress Press, 1996).

3. Bonhoeffer, *Life Together*, 53.

4. Ibid., 54–55.

5. Ibid., 53–60.

6. John Chapman, *Spiritual Letters* (New York: Burris & Oates, 2003), 109.

7. Thomas Merton, *New Seeds of Contemplation* (New York: New Directions, 1961), 31.

## 3   The Quiet Center

1. Thomas Merton, *Contemplative Prayer* (New York: Herder and Herder, 1969), 19–20.

2. Ibid., 66.

3. Henri Nouwen, *Making All Things New: An Invitation to the Spiritual Life* (New York: HarperOne, 1981), 70.

4. Ruth Burrows, *Essence of Prayer* (Mahwah, NJ: HiddenSpring/Paulist Press, 2006), 28, 31.

5. Thomas R. Kelly, *A Testament of Devotion* (New York: Harper & Brothers, 1941), 120.

6. June gave me permission to share her story and this e-mail, though I have changed her name.

7. Martin Laird, *Into the Silent Land: A Guide to the Christian Practice of Contemplation* (New York: Oxford University Press, 2006), 19. "The Wild Hawk of the Mind" is the title of chapter 2. More than any other approach to contemplative silence, Martin Laird's account in *Into the Silent Land* has influenced my approach in what follows. I'm deeply indebted to this book.

8. See, for example, the writings of John Main and Thomas Keating.

9. Henry D. Thoreau, *Walden: A Fully Annotated Edition*, ed. by Jeffrey S. Cramer (New Haven: Yale University Press, 2004), 1–2.

## 4   This Mortal Flesh

1. Quoted in Kathryn Spink, *The Miracle, The Message, The Story: Jean Vanier and L'Arche* (Mahwah, NJ: HiddenSpring/Paulist Press, 2006), 173.

2. Quoted in Rodney Clapp, "Bodily Blessing," *The Christian Century* (May 31, 2011): 37.

3. The retreat leader was Jane Vennard.

4. For a short account of this kind of prayer, see Jane E. Vennard, *A Praying Congregation: The Art of Teaching Spiritual Practice* (Herndon, VA: Alban Institute, 2005), 118–120.

5. Thomas Merton, *New Seeds of Contemplation* (New York: New Directions, 1961), 16.

6. Jane Vennard describes her morning prayer of intention in *The Praying Congregation*, 79. Upon rereading this, I see how greatly she influenced me.

## 5   Eat This Bread

1. *The United Methodist Book of Worship* (Nashville, TN: The United Methodist Publishing House, 1992), 37.

2. Ibid., 38.

3. Ibid., 39.

## 6   The Wounded Body of Christ

1. Peter Smith, "Presbyterian Church's Realignment Persisting: Numbers Slipping as Congregations Split," *Pittsburgh Post-Gazette* (June 3, 2014), www.post-gazette.com/local/region/2014/06/04/Presbyterian-Church-s-realignment-persisting/stories/201406040065, accessed October 2, 2014.

2. Burrows, *Essence of Prayer*, 170. "Asceticism of community" is my phrase.

3. Ibid., 169.

4. Ibid.

5. Benedict, *The Rule of St. Benedict in English,* ed. Timothy Fry (New York: Vintage Books, 1998), 8.

6. Dietrich Bonhoeffer, *Life Together*, 100–103.

7. Ibid., 100.

8. Ibid., 95.

9. Frederick Buechner, *Telling Secrets* (San Francisco: HarperSanFrancisco, 1991), 46. His description of the White Tower, which my description follows, is on pages 45–46.

10. Charles Wesley, "And Can It Be That I Should Gain," verse 4, in *The United Methodist Hymnal* (Nashville, TN: United Methodist Publishing House, 1989), no. 363.

11. Lesslie Newbigin, *The Open Secret: An Introduction to the Theology of Mission*, rev. ed. (Grand Rapids, MI: William B. Eerdmans, 1995), 48.

12. Bonhoeffer, *Life Together*, 109.

13. Parker J. Palmer, *A Hidden Wholeness: The Journey toward an Undivided Life* (San Francisco: Jossey-Bass, 2004), 58.

14. I wrote about Larry in the book, *Abba, Give Me a Word: The Path of Spiritual Direction* (Brewster, MA: Paraclete Press, 2012).

## 7 Unto the Least of These

1. Jonathan Wilson-Hartgrove, *New Monasticism: What It Has to Say to Today's Church* (Grand Rapids, MI: Brazos Press/Baker Publishing, 2008), 80.

2. Samuel Wells and Marcia A. Owen, *Living without Enemies: Being Present in the Midst of Violence* (Downers Grove, IL: InterVarsity Press, 2011), 23–40.

3. Ibid., 26.

4. Ibid., 30.

5. Thomas G. Long, *Matthew* (Louisville, KY: Westminster John Knox Press, 1997), 285.

6. Ibid., 285.

## In Closing

1. Gregory of Nyssa, *The Life of Moses*, trans. Abraham J. Malherbe and Everett Ferguson (New York: HarperOne, 2006), 106.

# ABOUT THE AUTHOR

L. ROGER OWENS is associate professor of leadership and ministry at Pittsburgh Theological Seminary, where he has taught since 2013. Before moving to Pittsburgh he copastored United Methodist churches in North Carolina with his wife, Ginger Thomas, for eight years. He is a frequent faculty presenter for The Upper Room's Academy for Spiritual Formation. He has written two other books including *Abba, Give Me a Word: The Path of Spiritual Direction*. He and Ginger are the parents of three children: Simeon, Silas, and Mary Clare.

Recommended by

# The Academy
## for spiritual Formation®
### THE UPPER ROOM

*for those who hunger for deep spiritual experience . . .*

THE ACADEMY FOR SPIRITUAL FORMATION is an experience of disciplined Christian community emphasizing holistic spirituality—nurturing body, mind, and spirit. The program, a ministry of The Upper Room, is ecumenical in nature and includes both lay and clergy persons. Each Academy fosters spiritual rhythms—of study and prayer, silence and liturgy, solitude and relationship, rest and exercise. With offerings of both Two-Year and Five-Day models, Academy participants rediscover Christianity's rich spiritual heritage through worship, learning, and fellowship. The Academy's commitment to an authentic spirituality promotes balance, inner and outer peace, holy living and justice living—God's shalom.

Faculty trained in the wide breadth of Christian spirituality and practice provide content and guidance at each session of The Academy. Academy faculty presenters come from seminaries, monasteries, spiritual direction ministries, and pastoral ministries or other settings and are from a variety of traditions. Author and theologian L. Roger Owens, a graduate of the Two-Year Academy, currently serves on The Academy advisory board and has served as faculty for The Academy for a number of years.

The ACADEMY RECOMMENDS program seeks to highlight content that aligns with The Academy's mission to provide resources and settings where pilgrims encounter the teachings, sustaining practices, and rhythms that foster attentiveness to God's Spirit and therefore help spiritual leaders embody Christ's presence in the world.

**Learn more at academy.upperroom.org**